Book of Colonial Needlework

Book of Colonial Needlework

A Handbook of Contemporary Projects:

Crewelwork / Whitework / Edgestitching / Faggoting / Drawnwork /
Stumpwork / Turkeywork / Candlewicking / Appliqué / Patchwork /
Hooking / Crochet / Braiding

Elizabeth J. Musheno

VNR VAN NOSTRAND REINHOLD COMPANY
New York   Cincinnati   Toronto   London   Melbourne

This book is dedicated to
Bonnibel Miller Quiggle Douty,
my mother,
and Minerva Weaver Miller,
my grandmother

Copyright © 1975 by Litton Educational Publishing, Inc.
Library of Congress Catalog Card Number 75-12166
ISBN 0-442-25607-8

Designed by Loudan Enterprises

Published in 1975 by Van Nostrand Reinhold Company
A Division of Litton Educational Publishing, Inc.
450 West 33rd Street
New York, NY 10001

Van Nostrand Reinhold Limited
1410 Birchmount Road
Scarborough, Ontario M1P 2E7, Canada

Van Nostrand Reinhold Australia Pty. Ltd.
17 Queen Street
Mitcham, Victoria 3132, Australia

Van Nostrand Reinhold Company Ltd.
Molly Millars Lane
Wokingham, Berkshire, England

16 15 14 13 12 11 10 9 8 7 6 5 4 3 2

Library of Congress Cataloging in Publication Data

Musheno, Elizabeth J
    Book of colonial needlework.

    Includes index.
    1. Needlework, American. 2. United States—
History—Colonial period, ca. 1600-1775. I. Title.
TT750.M87   746.4   75-12166
ISBN 0-442-25607-8

Appliqué and patchwork quilt. *Courtesy of the
Mount Vernon Ladies' Association. Photo: Marler.*

Acknowledgments

The printed word seems such an inadequate way to express my gratitude to the many people who helped make this book possible. Needlework is a fascinating and rewarding leisure-time vocation that has been enriched by the resources and cheerful assistance given so unselfishly; my sincere thanks to each person:

My husband, James, a tolerant soul who was often ignored as his wife pursued a "new love."

My daughters, Adelade Sullivan, Yvonne Leibrock, and Cathay Fulger—their skill and help in preparing the needlework projects for photography was immeasurable.

My editor, Nancy Newman, for her expert advice and sympathy.

The artists—Paige Camp, technical illustrator; Scott Hyde, photographer of the needlework projects; Lynn Ruthenberg, a typist who can read "chicken scratching."

Lib Calloway, who rekindled my interest in hooked rugs by her commonsense approach.

Museums and their designated staff members—Doris Bowman, the Smithsonian Institution; Ann Coleman, the Brooklyn Museum; the Metropolitan Museum of Art; Joanne Olean, the Museum of the City of New York; the Museum of Fine Arts, Boston; and the Concord Antiquarian Society.

Contents

A Brief Historical Introduction to Needlework

Entwined in the archives of our early American heritage are accounts of some of this nation's greatest benefactors—the dauntless colonial women. In spite of their diverse backgrounds all shared a common desire—religious or political freedom and the chance for a better way of life.

I-1 and I-2. Embroidered linen cape, front and back views. *Courtesy of the Smithsonian Institution.*

Those strong enough to survive the arduous journey to the New World were to endure many hardships before the land was cleared and their dwellings were built. Their isolation made it difficult, even for the affluent, to acquire basic supplies from Europe. These stalwart women had to make do with whatever they brought with them. Every article of clothing and household linen was remodeled, repaired, and reused. Recycling was a way of life for the colonists: every inch of fabric, yarn, or trimming was salvaged and used over again. Today's youth did not initiate this lifestyle when they started patching their blue jeans; neither did those enterprising persons who design and make new clothing and accessories out of usable sections of discarded denim garments. Recycling has been on the American scene since the Pilgrims arrived in the early 1600s. The colonists' frugal traits remained a part of our heritage until the 1940s, when American know-how began to supply our needs so quickly that we abandoned our thrifty habits and acquired the disposable syndrome prevalent today.

An artistic flair was evident as the womenfolk of the colonies undertook the colossal job of making clothing and bed covers to keep their families warm; rugs and curtains, to keep out the cold and decorate their drab and rough-hewn homes. When linens could not be mended invisibly, embroidery or appliqué designs were worked over the mended seams or stains. Clothing was trimmed wih decorative stitches to hide worn areas where hems were let down, or needlecrafted bands were added for length. Touches of brilliance and elegance satisfied the colonial woman's creative instincts when she needed a new petticoat or collar to spruce up a still good dress. All types of embroidery, quilting, rug making, and other needle arts were used to decorate the essential items needed for the family and home. As cloth items became worn beyond repair, still usable areas were carefully cut out and stored for future use. These scraps would reappear as new articles—an appliqué, a trimming—or would be used in numerous other ways, seen and unseen. Two original forms of needlecraft are attributed to these prudent women: patchwork quilts and hooked rugs. They were a natural development in their endeavor to use every precious bit of fabric.

Early American needlework ranged from sophisticated techniques to very plain stitchery. Some women learned their needlecraft skills abroad before coming to the colonies; others who did not have this advantage devised uncomplicated ways to enhance their homes with lovely practical items decorated with classic simplicity. These ardent women worked all year to collect materials to create new supplies from scratch; to spin, dye, and weave wool and flax in lengths of fabrics and yarns was hard work. It is difficult to imagine the planning required in these early days just to raise enough flax for household demands. After every successful harvest about a dozen different processes were needed to prepare the flax for spinning. Wool was somewhat easier to prepare, but still involved the transformation from fleece to cloth.

Today it is virtually impossible to be self-sustaining, as the early settlers were. Few Americans grow, harvest, and preserve their food, and very few are concerned directly with fuel for light, heat, or cooking. We do not have to make our clothing (unless we choose to do so), and we have a variety of homes, built by others, to choose from. In contrast, all early colonial families were totally independent—each family had its own land, built its own shelter, and was forced to supply all the food, fuel, light, clothing, and medicine required for its very existence.

There were no idle children in colonial America—each baby was welcomed as another pair of hands to help with the many chores. Even very young children were assigned tasks befitting their ability. Boys helped their fathers clear more land, collect wood for fuel, keep the home in repair, make new utensils and furniture, hunt and fish for meat, and tend and harvest the crops. Girls were kept busy learning how to cook, clean, preserve food, care for the sick, spin wool and linen thread, weave fabric, and make clothing and household articles from the "homespun."

A six-year-old girl could spin flax—and usually by her twelfth year she could set up a loom and weave simple fabrics. Four-year-old girls were taught to knit stockings and mittens; when a child mastered the heavier needles and yarn, she would use finer ones. Colonial young ladies frequently knitted elegant silk stockings (sometimes with designs or initials) to be worn with their wedding dresses.

Puritan morality as well as pioneer necessity drove the colonists. Hard work was a strict demand placed on the children—they were directed to keep busy to please the Lord so the Devil could not fill their heads with foolish or idle thoughts. Americans are considered the hardest workers in the world. And why not? It is a habit passed down from generation to generation for the two hundred years we have been a nation.

"Busywork" was given to every boy and girl who had chores, such as tending flocks in the field, that did not require total concentration. Such work might be "spinning-on-the-rock" (a term used by the colonial children when they spun threads with a distaff) or weaving tapes on simple heddle-frame looms as they walked along with the cattle and sheep. This spinning and weaving equipment was the same type used by Egyptians to spin linen threads and weave fabric strips to wrap mummies in.

As the colonies became prosperous, schooling was given to a greater number of children. Some were taught by their parents, others were tutored, and the well-to-do sent their children to England. Young George Washington and other Virginian children were sent to "old-field" schools—so called because they were unpretentious buildings constructed on the sites of old tobacco fields. Neighbors banded together to hire a teacher, but as soon as the children were able to read and master basic arithmetic, they were usually taken out of school. Later, as the colonies began to trade with other countries and life became easier, more girls went to school and learned more sophisticated types of needlework. Women settlers who embroidered were called "lazy squaws" by the Indians, who felt they should be working in the fields. The Indians did not condone the new freedom enjoyed by colonial women as they learned new ways to embellish their clothes and home furnishings with needlework.

A great camaraderie developed as the number of settlers increased with every ship that arrived. As self-made, independent people, the colonists were able to survive the most grueling experiences, and they were deeply concerned about and with each other. Every profession and trade was practiced in this new land. Each man developed competence in many areas—hunting, marksmanship, building, farming, and horsemanship. Women too contributed to colonial efforts to gain independence. In every village, town, and city women spun yarns and threads, wove cloth, and knitted. As early as 1640, the courts of Massachusetts offered a bounty for linen grown, spun, and woven in that colony—quantity and quality were rewarded with prizes.

As the demands for self-government increased, the Boston Commons became the scene of many "spinning parties" where women, rich and poor, brought their own spinning wheels to spin for the home guard. So precious was wool that sheep were allowed to graze on the Boston Commons. Their meat was not eaten to ensure a continuing supply of wool. If an uncontrolled dog killed a sheep, its owner had to pay the owner of the sheep twice the current market value of the sheep, and the dog was destroyed. Throughout the colonies English goods were boycotted—the "Daughters of Liberty" vowed to drink no tea and to wear only homespun garments. Spinning and weaving parties sponsored by the colonial ladies served as public forums as well. As their nimble fingers turned sheets, towels, and piece goods for clothing to supply the militia, they talked of resistance to the harsh laws being invoked by the English Crown. At sundown these patriotic women were joined by their husbands for the evening meal and the journey home.

With the combined efforts of every man, woman, and child, independence was worn for the colonies and a new era began. But the home crafts practiced as a survival measure were not discarded. Some were pursued with new vigor, and the techniques were refined as a greater variety of needlecraft supplies became available.

Have you ever wondered why men's vests are made the way they are? When ornate vests, such as the one shown in figure I-3, became fashionable, the fronts and flaps were embroidered on a length of fabric that was purchased from the Far East by way of England. Matching fabric for the vest backs was often not available, and by the time the vest was completed, it was impossible to find or dye the same color. Even whites were hard to bleach exactly the same shade each time. When the vest fronts were cut out, a compatible but different fabric back was extended along the sides and shoulders as far as needed to complete the vest. Today we still see the effects of this design feature created out of necessity—men's vests continue to have a front that matches the suit, with a lightweight back in a complementary fabric and color.

I hope that these historical notes will encourage women—and men—to pursue the time-honored needle arts described in this book, both those that have already been rediscovered and those that have nearly been forgotten. Directions for making basic accessories, garments, and items for the home are supplied to support your natural creativity. Every effort has been made to eliminate the mysteries of tools and materials so you can enjoy the serene pleasures of needlework inspired by our early American heritage.

I-3. Man's white linen vest with crewel embroidery. *Courtesy of the Smithsonian Institution.*

Chapter 1

A Simple Approach to Colonial Needlework

Through the years some of the needle arts that gave so much pleasure to the colonial women of America have remained favorites; others have faded out of sight, never again to achieve the status they previously enjoyed. You will find several "lost" favorites as well as the time-honored ones within these pages.

Any form of needlecraft—mending, sewing garments, knitting, crocheting, embroidering, doing needlepoint, making bed covers and other household items, quilting, or rug making—was "busywork." Busywork is not to be confused with "fancywork" (although fancywork can be busywork), which means any form of decorative needlecraft. Busywork was the simple act of always keeping one's hands busy while doing something else—waiting for the bread to rise or bake, traveling, talking with friends. Busywork was also a quiet respite from physical labor. The colonial woman would sit down to rest, but almost immediately she reached into her "pocket" to retrieve her busywork. The pocket was an apronlike container—an inventive piece of home craft constructed of two fabric layers, one of which was fancy, with a slit opening bound together along the side and lower edges with a tie-string at the top. Worn around the waist, it could be hidden under the folds of the overskirt when not in use and slid to the front, making her busywork easily accessible when she had a free moment or was visiting a friend. Using her own resources, the colonial woman learned to achieve peace of mind by keeping her hands and head busy; counting stitches and threads, along with the rhythm of her needle or hook, helped get rid of her frustrations.

Today busywork can play an equally important role. The rhythm of the needle provides relaxation more effective than a tranquilizer, and the things we make with our own hands give a special kind of emotional satisfaction.

1-1. Crewel-embroidered pockets, used by colonial women to carry their needlework. *Courtesy of the Smithsonian Institution.*

A Starting Point

Whether you have never used a needle or are a proficient embroiderer looking for new ways to expand your skills, you will need a starting point. "Think small" is the first precaution—many overeager novices have been swamped by a new endeavor in the needle arts because they selected a project too complicated or too involved for their limited skills.

No matter what your choice, explore the unknown with a small item first—potholders may sound dull, but as a gift to a friend who enjoys cooking, they are sheer delights. A seven-inch square will make a potholder and will give you a chance to test any of the needlecrafts.

If you are experienced with a needle, look for new ways to continue the therapeutic benefits derived from your favorite craft. Try elaborating on something you know how to do, or pick a completely new form. Some needleworkers find that flame-stitch, or bargello (a needlepoint embroidery stitch done on canvas by counting threads), requires too much concentration, while for others it's just what the doctor ordered. Some people may be comfortable with crochet or embroidery, but others will find sewing quilt blocks together more relaxing.

The three purses embellished with embroidery shown in color on page 82 are small, simple, and entirely handmade. They make excellent projects for the beginner, since a minimum amount of embroidery is required, and it can be as unpretentious or as elaborate as you desire. The embroidery used on the purse is representative of the many types you will find in this book: canvas embroidery for the flame-stitch pocketbook; stumpwork, using luxurious gold threads for couching, for the change purse; crewelwork appliqués, sewn on a velvet foundation, for the drawstring bag. (Instructions for making modified versions of the purses are found in Chapter 5.)

The flame-stitch man's pocketbook was made by Mary Little, who was born on November 16, 1749, and married Adams Bailer on June 17, 1779—it probably was her wedding gift to her new husband. Made from an embroidered seven-and-a-half- by ten-inch rectangle, it was bound and tied with green silk twill tape and lined with green silk.

The white silk change purse was made by working gold thread couching in a ribbon-and-bow design, and it originally had a handmade gold clasp. An interesting bit of history was revealed in a note tucked inside the purse by the donor.

This embroidered purse with solid gold clasp—on which 60$ was advanced, was at least as old as this casket (another gift, which was a small silver box with handle and screw key, made in 1650, belonging to the two wives of Thomas Tappan of Newberryport).

One very cold winter, after my husband went to India, I asked my friend Bigelow of Bigelow & Vunnard to advance its value upon it—that I might buy a necessary cloak & flannels, with the understanding that he should keep it until I could redeem it. The promise was made—but when three months after—I attempted to do so I found the promise forgotten and the clasp melted down. Bitterly did I regret that I had not borrowed the money instead. (C. H. Doll, 1837).

I have carefully preserved this embroidered purse, because *with* its gold clasp it was exactly like one exhibited in London a few years ago in a collection of articles which had belonged to Mary, Queen of Scots.

That (purse) is I suppose now in the possession of the widow of the Danish Architect, employed in the construction of the Crystal Palace in N.Y. Her name was Carstensen and she had a son in the 42nd St. Depot in 1879.

The blue velvet purse with a blue silk drawstring top was appliquéd with crewel embroidery worked on fine natural linen and was dated 1764. The velvet piece is about four inches by twelve inches.

The embroidered drawstring muslin workbag made with self-fringe and silk tassels, also shown on page 82, is an enlarged version of the drawstring bag, using a piece of muslin eighteen inches wide and thirty inches long.

These are just a few of the many easy but rewarding projects for anyone embarking on a new needlecraft. You can certainly add to the list all kinds of tote bags, place mats with matching napkins, pillows, pictures, and clothing accessories—the list is endless.

Pick an item that you would like to own or give away and set out to embellish it with embroidery or patchwork. Your enthusiasm and interest will carry you through any rough spots you may encounter.

Equipment, Storage, and Working Conditions

Again, my advice is "start small!" Take one step at a time. You may even have some useful equipment stashed away in the far corner of a top shelf in a closet. Most simple needlework requires only a few tools, and these usually take little space and are quite inexpensive.

1-2. Eighteenth- and nineteenth-century needlework tools and implements. *Courtesy of the Essex Institute, Salem, Massachusetts. Photo: Richard Merrill.*

Equipment

The most prized possessions of any needlecrafter are his tools and implements. Our ancestors were able to bring few personal possessions with them as they sailed to these virgin shores, but you can be sure that every woman considered her needles, thimble, and scissors a necessity—they were the basic tools for clothing her family. A collection of eighteenth- and nineteenth-century sewing equipment and needlework implements is shown in color on page 81. At the bottom, left to right, are scissors; buttonhole cotton; handmade rug hook; wooden crochet hook with bone top; and cast-iron "sewing bird" (a C-clamp with a serrated lever that held fabric and rug braids taut to speed up work). Just above are a silver thimble; bone afghan hook with wooden extension; and bone-handled extrafine crochet needle for making lace. Just above are a needle holder; extremely fine knitting needles, used to knit silk and very fine wool stockings, with their own hand-painted metal case; handmade awl; and pewter sewing bird with a spring clip. Left to right at the top are handmade straight pins, with the second paper of pins inscribed, "Pins Revolutionary Period 1775-1781 J. Calef." Many of the same tools are shown in figure 1-2.

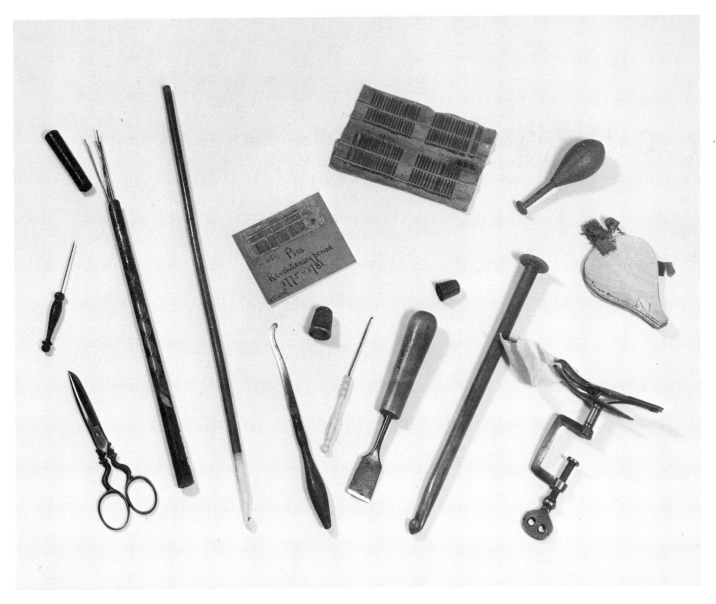

Needles

Colonial women carefully stored these precious slivers of metal and often kept favorite needles (bent to their particular needs from much use) for an entire lifetime. Today we have less regard for needles, as they can be purchased so easily and inexpensively. There are several types of needles, each with particular uses (figure 1-3).

Crewel (embroidery) needles are average in length, with large eyes and a sharp point, and are used with traditional embroidery threads and yarns. *Chenille* needles are shorter, with large, long eyes and a sharp point. They are easier to thread when you are using heavy yarns. *Tapestry* needles are average in length, with large eyes and a blunt point. They are used for counted-thread, canvas, and stumpwork embroidery. *Sharps* are the needles most women use for handsewing. Don't use too large a needle for your fabric; this will slow down your progress. Sizes 8 to 10 work best. Sharps are average in length, with a small eye and a sharp point. *Betweens* are used for handsewing and are the quilter's favorite—they are short, with small eyes and a sharp point.

Needles should be protected from dampness, as they may rust. Never stick them into the upholstery of the chair you are sitting in, and be sure to find one you drop on the floor—you may end up with it in your foot. Keep needles in a small box or pincushion, or make a little book with a flannel page to store them.

1-3.

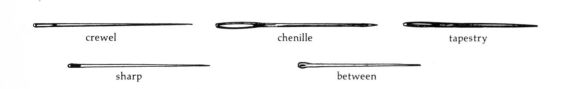

crewel   chenille   tapestry

sharp   between

Thimble

Learn to use one—it will prevent your middle finger from becoming sore (or even infected) when you use it to force the needle through the fabric and canvas. Be sure it fits correctly—it will help speed up your work.

Hooks—Rug and Crochet

You will need these hooks to make the sock rug and the hooked rug described in Chapter 4. A jumbo crocket hook, size Q, is needed to make the sock rug, and a rug hook with a wooden handle is needed for the hooked rug.

Scissors

A well-forged pair of scissors, five to seven inches long, with points that close properly and cut to the tip, is essential for all-purpose use. Every needlecraft has a few preparatory steps that involve cutting. Foundation fabric and canvas must be cut to size for embroidery; quilt patches and blocks need to be cut out before they can be sewn together; and yards of strips need to be cut from fabric or socks to make a rug. These same scissors may be used to snip threads and yarn ends as you embroider, quilt, or sew by hand. As you progress, a three-and-a-half-inch-long pair of embroidery scissors will lighten your load when you carry needlework about, work with a hoop or frame, and make a quilt or rug.

Pins

Every needleworker needs a variety of pins to fasten patterns to fabric or to hold layers together at different stages of a project. Fine, sharp silk pins (size 17) are essential for every workbasket, and size 24 pins work well when pinning heavy layers together, as they are longer and thicker. T-pins are used with a padded frame and to pin quilts and comforters together during construction.

Hoops and Frames

These two items help to keep your work from puckering or pulling out of shape. (There are few types of needlecraft that cannot be done in your lap—they will be indicated when the procedure is explained.) Round hoops with a thumbscrew work fine for many projects, but when you are making something with a raised surface, pad around the raised area with tissue paper when the hoop is slipped in place to avoid flattening the stitchery.

To use a hoop, place the smaller ring on a flat surface and lay the work over it; place the larger ring down over the work and tighten the screw. If your fabric becomes loose, be sure to pull it tight on the straight grain; pulling on the bias may distort the design and pucker the threads. There are many types of hoops—choose the one that will do the best job for you (figure 1-4). A simple pair with a thumbscrew works best for beginners—all needlecrafters use it because it is portable and requires little space. For large projects use one of the freestanding, floor, table, clamp, or fanny (there's a base that you sit on, making it portable) hoops. These freestanding hoops allow you to adjust the height and angle so you can use both hands, thus speeding up the work.

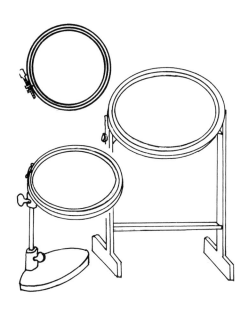

1-4.

Frames also come in many sizes and types. They may require a place to support one edge or be freestanding. They can be as elaborate or as simple as you desire. The most practical (and economical) frame is one made of artists' stretcher strips hammered together gently, with the corners square. Use the wooden wedges to hold the frame together permanently or fasten each corner with tacks. Make a square or rectangle to suit your particular needs—a fourteen-inch square will slide into a shopping bag easily; a sixteen- by twenty-inch frame gives you more working area. Your work can be held in place with pushpins, but a padded frame with T-pins is recommended for the projects in this book.

To make a padded frame, use artists' stretcher frames as directed above or a sturdy picture frame. Cut three-inch-wide fabric strips from a used garment, old sheet, or muslin. If your fabric is quite thin, double the strips. Wrap each side with the fabric strips, leaving the corners uncovered—they are difficult to wrap and are never used (figure 1-5). To start, fasten the fabric strip on one side with staples or tacks. Wrap several layers of fabric over the staples to form a cushion of padding. Continue wrapping the wooden side of the frame as you would a bandage, making strip edges about half an inch apart. If the fabric strip is not long enough to cover one side of the frame, lap the end of the second strip over the end of the first and fasten both securely. Continue until the side is wrapped, fastening the fabric end securely. Do the same for each side.

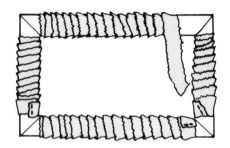

1-5.

To anchor your work with T-pins, place the work over the frame, making sure that one side and one edge of the design are free of the inner frame edges. Pulling the fabric taut as you go, place a T-pin at the center of each frame side. Next, anchor each side with more pins, working from the center pin to each end (five or seven pins on each side works best). Do the top and bottom in the same manner.

To support the padded frame, place one edge on a table, stand, TV snack tray with legs, or chair back the proper height for you. My granddaughter, Beth Sullivan (age 8), hooks a pillow top as she sits on the floor watching TV. She finds the lower level of an end table perfect for her.

Storage

There's no need to make a big thing out of storage—the early American needlecrafter put her equipment in cloth bags and hung them on the walls or rafters of her home. There are many ardent craftsmen who simply store their supplies in shopping bags, pushed to the back of a closet. With space at a premium in small apartments or mobile homes, many things are stored in boxes under the bed. Let's face it—craftsmen are packrats and will find a place to store their goodies while working on another project. Just be sure to mark each container clearly to avoid undue searching.

Fabric and Canvas

The safest way to store any kind of fabric is rolled. With linen, burlap, and canvas it is essential to prevent the fibers from breaking. Gift-wrapping-paper rolls taped together, mop or broom handles, or other round objects that are at least as wide as the fabric will do. Other less fragile fabrics can be folded and stored in a box. Cover your rolls with plastic or paper bags and anchor with tape for protection.

Yarns and Threads

There are so many see-through plastic bags and boxes on the market that storage is much easier than it was in years gone by. Small sandwich bags are perfect for cotton embroidery floss and some of the tapestry yarns; larger bags are useful for threads and yarns in longer shanks. You can separate each color or all the shades of one color for one type of thread, and then store each set together in one container.

Tools

Store small items that you use frequently in a special place. Why not make your own needlework carrier with a place for embroidery scissors, thimble, and needles; a special pocket for your current project; and a place for your yarn and thread? A simple shopping bag with a small box for your tools and a plastic bag to protect everything else is quite adequate. Hoops and frames should be covered while stored. If you take them apart, tape any nuts or screws to one of the sections to avoid losing them. All needles, hooks, and other metal implements should be stored in a dry place to prevent rust.

Working Conditions

The beauty of needlework is that it's portable (unless you have designed large sections to be decorated)—just about any place is the spot to pursue your favorite pastime. Many needlecrafters have two or more projects going at the same time and change back and forth for variety. This way they are never discouraged, and, when the retired project is picked up again, it is completed with dispatch. Commuters may embroider, knit, or crochet en route to their jobs but find quilting relaxing after a busy day.

For many needlecrafters a comfortable chair and a good light is all they require for a place to work. Others even find a seat on a racing subway train quite adequate. Outgoing people like a lively conversation and prefer a spot surrounded by friends—indoors or out. People mesmerized by TV would do themselves a favor if they did a little busywork as they watched.

Fabrics, Threads, and Yarns

Modern technology provides an ever-increasing supply of new fabrics and fibers. Some may not be satisfactory for needlework; others are superior. Some materials will withstand frequent laundering; others must never be touched with water. When making your selections, be sure to match the durability of your materials with the needs of your project. A woman's evening dress will receive much less wear than an active child's pinafore: choose the fabric for each accordingly.

For Embroidery

Fabrics, yarns, and threads suitable for embroidery cover a wide range. Any fabric from the sheerest lightweight fabric to heavyweight home-spuns may be used for the foundation. Yarns and threads may be so fine that they are almost hairlike or thick and fluffy; they may be made from fibers of precious gold or simple cotton. Whatever your whim, the choice is challenging.

Fabrics

Nearly any fabric can be enhanced by embroidery—some will require more time than others when transferring the design (see below), but the efforts are worth it. Linen, muslin, and synthetic linenlike fabrics are still the first choice of most embroiders—the threads are easily separated and penetrated. To prevent the fabric from fraying, it is wise to turn the edges under half an inch and baste them in place.

Yarns and Threads

The same type of three-ply Persian yarn used for thousands of years by needleworkers when they made rugs and wall hangings for kings and queens is still available. Many ardent needlepointers will use nothing else. Some wool, silk, and linen yarns and threads used for crewelwork and many other ancient types of embroidery have changed little through the years. Any smoothly twisted or plied thread or yarn that can be easily threaded through a needle and pulled through the fabric may be used for your embroidery. You are limited only by your imagination: gold and silver, cotton, silk, wool, and the wonderful synthetics are available.

For Quilts and Comforters

Always select quality new or recycled materials. It would be unwise to spend your time and effort on less than satisfactory supplies.

Fabrics

Firmly woven, smooth, nonraveling fabrics that feel soft to the touch work best. Purchase preshrunk fabric; shrink unknowns. Try calico, gingham, polished cotton, broadcloth, or any of the cotton blends that emulate these cotton fabrics. Muslin, natural or bleached, is still a favorite, but it needs to be shrunk.

Batting

Cotton is the traditional stuffing for quilts, but it must be closely quilted to prevent lumping. Polyester batting, a wonderful modern material, needs less surface quilting, as it holds its shape. Only polyester batting should be used for the knotted comforter in Chapter 3, whose surface has large areas that are not anchored.

A faded wool blanket or a flannel sheet blanket makes a nice substitute for batting. But please note: dark-colored blankets may show through white or light-colored quilt blocks. And remember that the thinner the batting is, the easier it will be to quilt.

Thread and yarn

Strong white cotton thread, sizes 40 to 50, or a cotton-covered polyester core works best for quilting. Use beeswax to prevent tangling: pull each thread length over the beeswax several times before threading it into the needle. This coats the thread with a light film of wax, making it firmer and keeping it from twisting or knotting—use beeswax for all handsewing. Knitting worsted and crochet cotton are used to knot comforters.

For Rugs

The traditional fabric for rugs was wool. Today, choose the fiber best suited to your needs. Both braided and hooked rugs work best with medium-weight wool-flannel-type fabrics. Knits may be used for braided rugs. Burlap is used as a foundation for hooked rugs. But a word of caution: colored burlaps are not satisfactory for hooking, as a combination of fibers is used that will not withstand the wear. Use tightly woven natural burlap that has firm, round threads.

Canvas

Embroidery canvas is an unusual fabric that is loosely woven with evenly spaced, rounded threads. Hemp, flax, and cotton fibers have been used for many centuries, but today the threads are treated with chemicals, making the canvas superior to that used by the colonial women. There are two types of canvas. Mono (single-thread) canvas comes in all mesh sizes, from the finest gauze to eight meshes to the inch; penelope (double-thread) canvas is available in mesh sizes from five to fourteen meshes to the inch. (There is also an evenly spaced, twisted, double-thread rug canvas that was not known to the early American rug maker and is not suitable for the projects in this book.)

Designs Are Where You Find Them

Design is a stumbling block for many would-be needleworkers. Kits are a common solution to the problem of *what* to embroider, hook, sew, etc.— but if you can free yourself from your fear of design, you will find yourself so much freer to create. Don't be afraid that what you draw will be too awkward. Look at the designs of the colonial women. They were not trained artists: they were not concerned with perspective or scale but simply drew the forms that pleased them, the objects in their surroundings— animals, nature, people. If figurative design still terrifies you, try geometric motifs—anyone can draw a series of circles, squares, and lines. (They don't have to be exact—remember, the work is *hand*made. Or go to simple designs that you can copy: the border on a roll of paper towels, one of your children's drawings, a picture from a coloring book.

Colonial women were inspired by their new surroundings. The petticoat with the crewel band shown in figure 5-22 was made in Vermont in the eighteenth century. The trees and animals are excellent examples of simple, pleasing designs. Don't be afraid to call upon a husband, wife, child, or friend to help create a design for needlework. Many of the designs used by the colonial women were drawn by their menfolk. These great ladies also shared their designs with their friends—it was considered an honor to have an acquaintance copy your work.

As you look for designs, notice how many of the finest examples of colonial needlecraft are decorated with that old standby, the chain stitch. The well-preserved white linen vest shown in figure I-3 was embroidered with a scroll, using two rows of shaded chain stitches. The leaf side of the scroll was made with darker shades of the same color.

How to Enlarge Designs

Start with easy, uncomplicated designs and soon you will be creating imaginative, original patterns that your friends will want to borrow. The easiest way to start is with a design the exact size of the piece you want to do. You can make a pattern by tracing it on artists' tracing paper, which comes in sheets or on a roll in many sizes and widths. Tissue paper or any other thin paper will also work. (If your source of inspiration is a snapshot, a fabric motif, or a picture in a book, put a sheet of clear, stiff plastic or a pane of glass between the tracing paper and the original so as not to mar the original.)

Most often, however, the design you choose will not be the size you need in your work, and you will have to enlarge it (figure 1-6). Use a sheet of paper (artists' tracing paper, shelf or wrapping paper) slightly larger than the desired size, a ruler, and a sharp pencil. Decide on the scale of enlargement you want for your project. The standard scale is one to four—one-quarter inch enlarged to one inch—but work out the proportions that best suit your work. Tape the original small design to a hard, flat surface and draw equal lines lightly over its surface, forming squares (1). Now tape the large sheet of paper in place and draw as many large squares as you have small squares in the proportion you have selected. Draw in the design lines lightly in each corresponding enlarged square (2). When the entire design is transposed, add your own personal touch as you smooth out lines and refine the design.

Throughout the book you will find pictures and designs you may wish to enlarge in this manner. If you are working with large overall designs, make a single enlargement for each pattern repeat and use it as often as needed.

1-6.

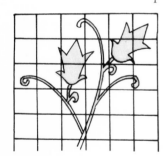

each square = 1 inch

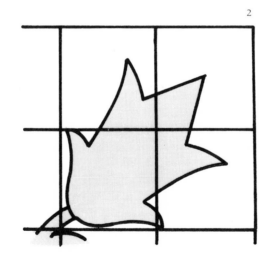

Transferring Designs to Fabric

There are many methods of transferring designs, but not all methods will work for all fabrics. Some fabrics may be damaged by the heat from an iron or the pressure of a sharp pencil. *Always test your selected method on a fabric scrap before starting.* Textured weaves and fabrics with thick-and-thin thread create problems, as do napped fabrics, so be careful.

Dressmakers' Carbon

Carbon is a very convenient form of transferring, as it comes in light and dark colors. Graphite paper, which can be purchased at artist-supply stores, works well too, but typing-paper carbon smudges.

Place the fabric right side up on a smooth, hard surface and tape it in place. Lay the carbon paper face down on the fabric and tape or pin. Center the pattern face up on top of the carbon; tape or pin to hold it in place. Transfer the design lines to the fabric with a hard, sharp-pointed pencil, checking to see that you are using enough pressure for legible lines.

Hot-Iron Transfers

There are a number of commercial designs available that can be transferred by this method, and many embroiderers like to use them rather than creating their own. Follow the instructions carefully.

Wax crayons are an old standby—they work well on light-colored, smooth fabric but are appropriate for crewel embroidery *only*, as the colors tend to spread. Trace the reverse side of your pattern with the darker shades, keeping the points sharp. Pin or tape the fabric to the ironing board, position the pattern (crayon side down), and secure. Place the iron over the design—do not slide it, but lift it up and down gently.

Pencil or Pen Transfers

This method works well on rough or textured fabrics. Tape the fabric right side up to a smooth, hard surface. Center the design over the fabric and tape or pin. With a sharp, medium-soft lead pencil, ballpoint, or fine-point felt-tip pen, pierce the paper with the point, making dots as close together as required to show the outline clearly.

Basting Transfers

If you are determined to embroider a design directly on velvet or any napped fabric, it can be done. Place the paper pattern on the wrong side of the fabric and baste in place with long running stitches. Transfer the outline to the right side of the fabric with short basting stitches. When the entire outline is traced, gently tear away the pattern, making sure you do not pull out the stitches. Embroider the design, then remove the basting stitches.

Chapter 2

Embroidery Then and Now

Embroidery certainly was not a commodity which affected the economic and political stability of the colonies, like weaving and spinning; little is recorded about its popularity. However, we are cognizant of many authentic examples that were carefully preserved, some dating back to the middle 1600s. Some Puritan women probably brought needlework on board the *Mayflower* to pass the time as they sailed to a new life across the Atlantic Ocean. Crewel embroidery, such as that used for the slipcover shown in figure 2-1, had long been a favorite in England, and supplies were plentiful. In packing essential clothing, household equipment, and linens for her new home, the ardent needlecrafter probably included a few precious skeins of crewel-embroidery wool, a small selection of patterns, and maybe a short length of fabric, in spite of the limited space allotted to each family.

When they arrived on these shores, the new settlers had little time to pursue the more ornate forms of needlecraft. The activities necessary to sustain life were strenuous and time-consuming, and for a long time the necessary materials were not available. Although colonial women admired the porcupine-quill embroidery of the American Indians, with its beautiful geometrics and flying designs created with dyed animal quills and deerskin, it was considered too primitive—they still had memories of beautifully embroidered garments and linens. As soon as the sheep herds (which were brought with them on the *Mayflower*) increased substantially, embroidery wool was made, imitating as nearly as possible the twists and plies of the wool made in England.

Embroidery is one of the oldest needle arts. Although it is generally considered to be a feminine avocation, as early as the thirteenth century men were making fine ecclesiastical embroidery. Today, contemporary men have become avid needleworkers as we move into an era when nearly every vocation or handicraft is enjoyed by both women and men.

2-1. Linen slipcover for a wing chair with crewel embroidery, from New England, 1750–75. *Courtesy of the Museum of Fine Arts, Boston. Gift of Miss Ellen W. Coolidge.*

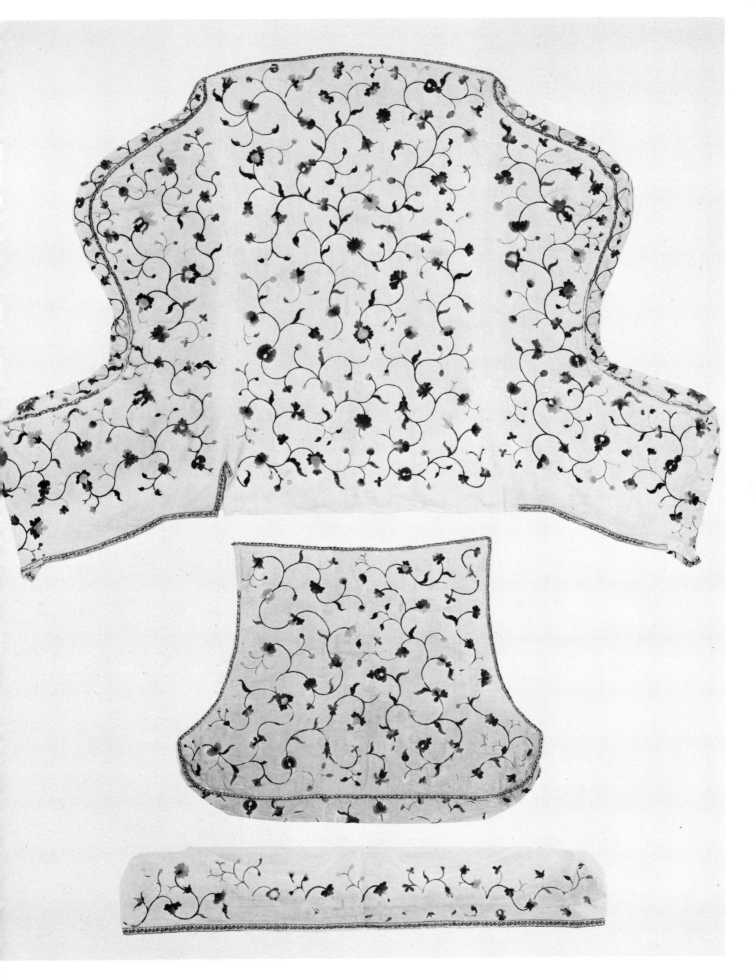

Types of Embroidery

The broad spectrum covered by the term "embroidery" is phenomenal: it includes any decorative stitch on a fabric foundation. Embroidery can decorate a surface, create a pattern of holes in a fabric, or trim an edge with stitches.

Crewelwork employs two mediums: wool yarn for the embroidery thread and linen or linenlike cottons and wools for the foundation fabric. The wool yarn can be single- or multiple-ply, and the foundation fabric can be as lightweight as handkerchief linen or as heavyweight as the linsey-woolsey homespun used to make the colonial bed rugs.

This oldest form of needle art can be as sophisticated or as simple as you desire. However, one thing is certain—crewel embroidery can become addictive. Just watch that handsome young man sitting next to you on the bus working eagerly as he fills in another motif on his own original design, or two happy young girls comparing projects to see who has completed the most—it can become a madness!

Stumpwork is embroidery with an added dimension—a raised surface is built up with thread or a padded appliqué, and detached embroidery stitches are worked over it. In England sharp bits of wood were used to create raised areas, often with faces painted on the stumps of wood. This may be the origin of the term.

Many lovely *openwork* techniques are making a comeback as American clothing designers incorporate some of the lost needle arts to commemorate the bicentennial. *Insertion* stitches, such as faggoting, and *drawn thread-work*, often called *hemstitching*, like so many other fine needlecrafts, can now be duplicated by machine. Handmade openwork changes a simple garment into a haute-couture design. Nothing can be more beautiful than the hand-worked detail of hemstitching and other embroidery done over the open spaces of fabrics in which threads have been removed.

Many basic embroidery stitches can be used to create interesting open-work simply by pulling the stitches tight on loosely woven fabric. This type of embroidery, known as *drawn fabricwork*, is not to be confused with the drawn-thread technique used to make hemstitching.

Whitework is surface embroidery or openwork done on white fabric with white threads and yarns. It is still considered the most dramatic form of embroidery for handkerchiefs, linens, or accessories such as collars and cuffs. Delicate edgings made by incorporating embroidery stitches are often found on whitework and handmade lingerie.

Another form of whitework utilizes the lofty, tufted *candlewick stitches*, which have almost disappeared. This needle art was given its name because some inventive eighteenth-century woman substituted candlewick yarn for the traditional embroidery thread used in England.

Two of the most popular canvas-embroidery techniques, needlepoint and bargello, have remained timeless favorites, while another, turkey-work, passed out of favor by the end of the eighteenth century.

Needlepoint is a method of embroidery in which the foundation is completely covered. Diagonal stitches are worked over the intersecting canvas threads in a variety of patterns. This form of needle art is one of the most durable and will withstand years of hard use even on upholstery, handbags, and pillows. The stitch most widely used in colonial times was the tent stitch (sometimes called petit point). Martha Washington was the most famous early American woman known for her devotion to needle-point. In spite of the great demands on her time, both as the wife of a prominent political figure who liked to entertain and as the mistress of a large plantation, she practiced many needle arts. Some historians feel this remarkable woman was a slow worker—she took nearly twenty-five years to needlepoint twelve chair-seat covers—but those of us who pursue the art consider it an outstanding accomplishment. George was away from Mount Vernon for months at a time, leaving the management of the estate entirely up to her. Not only did she direct the making of clothes for everyone on the plantation, but she often laid out the patterns for cutting. She also liked to piece quilts (see Chapter 3). Martha Washington approached needlecraft as many of us still do—she always had one continuing project (such as the twelve shell-design chair covers) that she interspersed with others, often out of necessity. She was still doing her favorite needlework after her seventieth birthday.

Bargello differs from needlepoint in that stitches are worked vertically over four threads, while needlepoint stitches are worked diagonally. It is possible to transfer a design to canvas in needlepoint, but bargello is worked from a graph, and the threads are carefully counted to establish the pattern. The top edge of the design pattern must be centered on the top outline of the work.

A simple slipknot formed by taking two backstitches over adjoining threads on the canvas is the method used to form a lush pile embroidery called *turkeywork*. Early settlers were inspired by the beautiful carpets imported to the colonies via England from Turkey. Some designs were worked on heavy hemp canvas, as the settee shown in color on page 83, while others were worked on heavy woolen homespun and used as bed covers.

The story of embroidery is just beginning—with hoop, needle, and thread in hand it would be an exhilarating experience for you to test some of the lovely stitches you are about to learn. Why not make a sampler as our foremothers did? Some early samplers, like the one shown on page 81, were "working" samplers. They show how the needleworker's techniques improved—some stitches were quite elegant, others somewhat irregular. The wide interest of this embroiderer was shown by the many types she practiced: bargello and filling stitches, openwork, cross-stitches with several styles of initials (some worked in reverse), and the beautiful "tree-of-life" pattern with Adam, Eve, a child, birds, deer, a dog, a horse, a house, religious symbols, and flowers.

Samplers were really the needlewoman's workbook to record stitches she enjoyed making. Because of this, the samplers lacked composition—patterns were practiced at the whim of the worker. Later, samplers were used to teach letters and numbers to small girls and were arranged symmetrically, balanced by decorative motifs, and framed with a border.

Are the ideas starting to swirl in your head? I surely hope so. Now, let's move on to the real thing.

Crewelwork

This needle art has been held in high esteem ever since women began painting beautiful pictures with worsted yarn. The beautiful bedspread shown in figures 2-2 through 2-5 may well serve as an inspirational example.

There are two ways to form crewel stitches—the method you select is determined by the foundation fabric and the embroidery yarn or thread. For supple, loosely woven fabrics the stitches are sewn, a procedure just like handsewing. Stitches that are worked on crisp, delicate, or very heavy fabrics using yarns or threads that are firm and unyielding are made with a stabbing technique: the needle is taken to the back through the fabric and then reinserted to the front to form each stitch. All crewelwork stitches may be done both ways: the fabric and the yarn are always the deciding factors. When the materials selected do not present a problem, use the method that is the most comfortable for you.

2-2, 2-3, 2-4, and 2-5. Linen bedspread with crewel embroidery, made in 1772. *Courtesy of the Brooklyn Museum. Gift of the Misses Latimer.*

For any stitch the first step is to thread the needle. Squash the yarn between your thumb and first finger and slide it into the needle (figure 2-6). Form a knot at one end (figure 2-7) by wrapping the thread around the first finger, then crossing the thread end to form an X (1). Place your thumb over the crossed threads, holding the yarn taut. Gently roll the yarn to form a loop and slide it off your fingertip (2). Pull the yarn taut as you hold the loop with your fingernail against your thumb to form the knot (3).

To end a thread anywhere in your work, take several stitches in an area that will be covered or turn the work over and weave the thread around several stitches.

Use a hoop and a sharp-pointed needle for all stitches unless otherwise instructed.

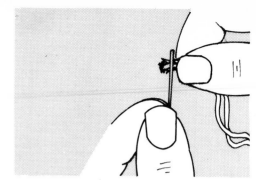

2-6.

2-7.

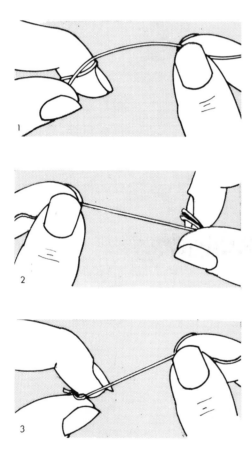

Backstitch

This stitch is used for outlines and borders. Working from right to left, bring the needle out through the fabric. Insert the needle behind the yarn and bring it out an equal distance ahead of the yarn (figure 2-8).

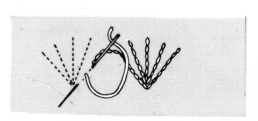

2-8.

Outline Stitch

This stitch is worked from left to right or backward along the design lines. Bring the needle to the outside, then take a stitch to the right, keeping the thread above the needle (figure 2-9).

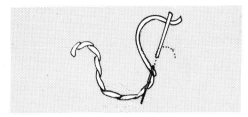

2-9.

Stem Stitch

This stitch is also worked from left to right or backward along the design lines. Bring the needle to the outside and take a stitch to the right, keeping the thread below the needle (figure 2-10). The shorter the stitch, the more the twist will be apparent.

2-10.

Split Stitch

This stitch was used in shades of brown in figure 2-58 to fill in the fence. Use a soft thread for the best effect. Working from left to right or backwards, bring the needle to the surface of the fabric. Take a stitch, splitting the thread as it emerges from the fabric (figure 2-11).

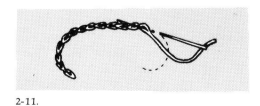

2-11.

Satin Stitch

This stitch can be done in two different ways (figure 2-12). The first method uses as much yarn on the reverse side of the embroidery as on the top. Bring the needle to the outside, take a stitch at the opposite edge, and carry the thread over and under the design (1). The second method uses less yarn, as only a tiny stitch shows on the underside. Bring the needle to the outside, take a tiny stitch (picking up only one thread) on the opposite design edge, and carry the thread across the design (2). The secret is to place the stitches close together, creating a smooth, embroidered surface. Of course, this requires some practice.

2-12.

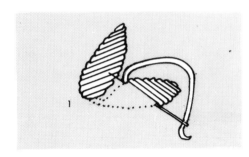

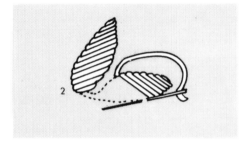

Long-and-Short Stitch

This stitch is used to fill in designs with texture and shading (figure 2-13). It is worked in the same manner as the first method of the satin stitch.

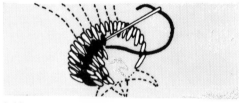

2-13.

Brick Stitch

This stitch is a precisely made running stitch, alternated in each row to look like the bricks on a building (figure 2-14). Make stitches half an inch long or less, picking up a thread or two, with a sixteenth-inch space between each stitch. It can be worked in either direction.

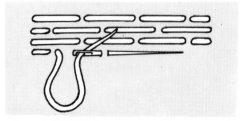

2-14.

French Knot

This stitch was used to form the flowers in the cape shown in figures I-1 and I-2. Bring the thread to the outside. Grasp it firmly with one hand and wind it around the needle several times. Reinsert the needle very close to where it emerged, holding the thread taut along the fabric and the loop close to the needle. Pull the thread through the loops, forming a knot on the surface (figure 2-15).

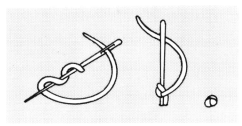

2-15.

Simple Buttonhole Stitch

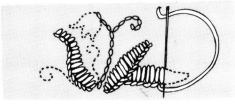

2-16.

A variation of the blanket stitch used in edgestitching (figure 2-53), this stitch is used to fill in designs, to outline, and for openwork. Work from left to right, bringing the needle to the outside of the outer line of the design. Holding the thread down with your thumb, insert the needle slightly to the right of where it emerged on the inner line and bring it out on the outer line over the thread loop (figure 2-16).

Vandyke Stitch

This stitch was used by many colonial women to save yarn. The petticoat shown in figure 5-22 relied on this stitch almost exclusively. Shape the outer edges but keep the twist at the center. The enlarged stitch is the foundation: bring the needle up at the edge of the design; take a stitch from right to left slightly above this point at the center. Take a tiny stitch along the right edge of the design. Now, from left to right, insert the needle under the crossed center but not into the fabric, then take a tiny stitch along the left edge of the design. Insert the needle under the next pair of crossed threads, moving from right to left. Continue alternating in this manner until the design is filled in (figure 2-17).

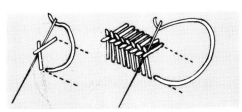

2-17.

Chain Stitch

Bring the thread to the outside and form a loop. Holding the loop down with your thumb, insert the needle in the same spot where it just came out and take a short stitch, keeping the loop under the needle. Pull up the thread, shaping the loop as desired. A chain will form as you follow the design lines, repeating the same procedure for each loop or link (figure 2-18). The handsome chain-stitch designs shown in figures 2-19 and 2-20 illustrate the great versatility of this simple stitch. Notice the lazy-daisy stitch on the fernlike spray of chain stitch: the loops are pulled so tight that they look like a single thread in some places.

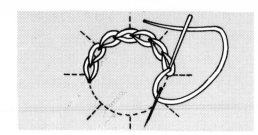

2-18.

Lazy-Daisy Stitch

This is a separated version of the chain stitch used to make petals and small leaves. Bring the thread to the outside and form a loop. Holding the loop down with your thumb, insert the needle in the same spot. Take a stitch, keeping the loop under the needle, and anchor the loop with a tiny stitch (figure 2-21).

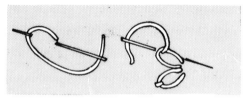

2-21.

Ladder Stitch

This is an open chain stitch worked along two lines. It is used for borders and outlines. Bring the thread to the outside on the bottom line. Form a loop with the thread and hold it down with your thumb. Insert the needle into the top line opposite the thread on the bottom line and take a stitch, keeping the loop under the needle at an angle to the bottom line (figure 2-22). Keep the thread loose on the fabric, not pulled taut. Make the spaces (rungs) uniform, making stitches as close together or as far apart as desired.

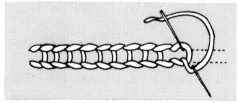

2-22.

Feather Stitch

This stitch was used for the delicate border on the embroidered linen cape shown in figures I-1 and I-2. Bring the thread to the outside at the top of the design. Take a stitch to the right of the line, forming a loop, and keep the loop under the needle. Make a stitch from the left in the same manner, covering the line with part of the loop (figure 2-23).

2-23.

Fern Stitch

Simple fernlike leaves are made by working three stitches of the same length, all of which emerge from the same hole (figure 2-24).

2-24.

Cross-Stitch

This stitch must be worked on a fabric with countable threads, one to which a design can be transferred precisely, or one printed with spaces, such as gingham. Work from right to left, inserting the needle vertically from top to bottom to form one bar of the X. Then work from left to right, inserting the needle in the same holes to form a row of completed cross-stitches (figure 2-25).

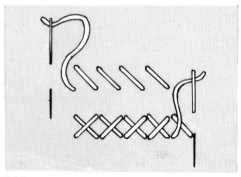

2-25.

Seed Stitch

Tiny, straight stitches worked in pairs may be used to fill in a design with a scattered look. Seed stitches may also be used with shades of one color in straight lines (figure 2-26).

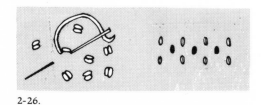

2-26.

Openwork

The term "openwork" connotes several types of embroidery that create holes or openings in the fabric. Colonial women used these stitches most effectively to make linen baby caps, stoles, handkerchiefs, and dresses. In the late eighteenth century when the empire silhouette was introduced, hemstitching, one form of openwork, was used to make wedding dresses. The fragment of white linen shown in figure 2-27 probably came from such a garment. The baby caps in figure 2-28 show several classic varieties of openwork and whitework. The head kerchief in figure 2-29 combines cutwork and drawn fabricwork with crewelwork.

2-27. Fragment of a late eighteenth-century dress with hemstitching and crewel embroidery. *Courtesy of the Smithsonian Institution.*

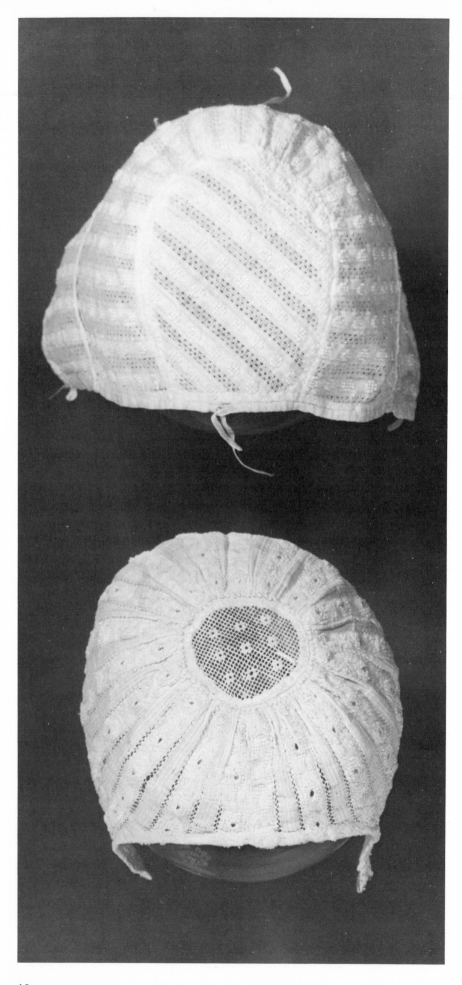

2-28. White linen baby caps, embroidered with crewelwork, cutwork, drawn fabricwork, and drawn threadwork. *Courtesy of the Smithsonian Institution.*

Openwork, as you can see, is done in many ways. Some are quite simple, while others are more complex. The selection offered here includes those stitches that can be used most effectively by the contemporary needlecrafter. Fabric selection is most important for all types of openwork embroidery. Use only quality fabric that is crisp and loosely woven in a plain, even weave. All weights of linen and muslin, homespun-type cottons and wools, and some transparent organdies and voiles are good. Threads should complement the fabric but need not be the same material. Cotton, linen, silk, or wool floss and threads may be used. In colonial times some of this embroidery was done with self-threads or homespun threads. Self-threads were unraveled from the fabric edges or withdrawn from the fabric to make openings for hemstitching. After the homespun threads were bleached, several skeins were set aside for embroidery. When the fabric was woven, the needlecrafter had perfectly matched thread for any openwork project.

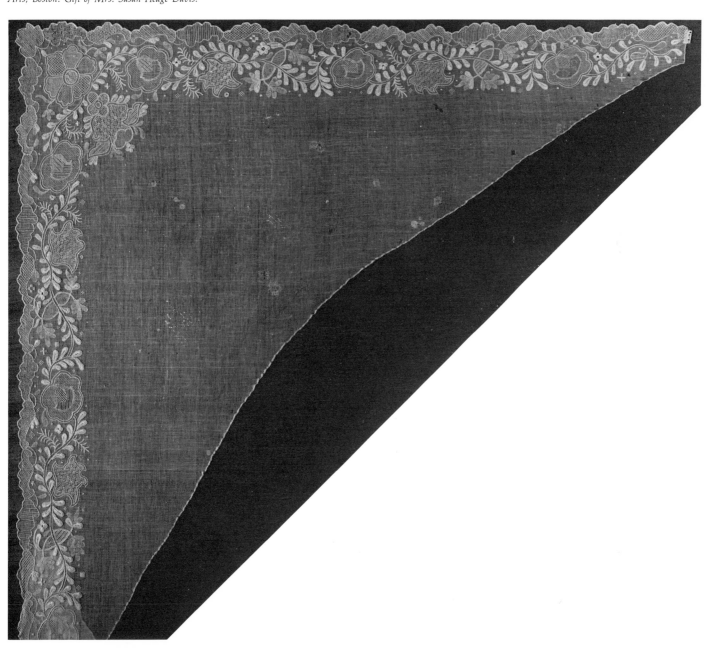

2-29. Gauze muslin kerchief, embroidered with cutwork, drawn fabricwork, and crewelwork, made by Rachael Leonord, Norton, Massachusetts, dated 1752. *Courtesy of the Museum of Fine Arts, Boston. Gift of Mrs. Susan Hedge Davis.*

Drawn Threadwork or Hemstitching

In this technique threads are removed from the fabric to create openings, while the remaining threads are embroidered. The stitches do not have to be used for hems: beautiful openwork has also been created with drawn threads that are *not* hemmed with the embroidery.

Use a hoop and a blunt-pointed needle to make all of these stitches. Threads can be pulled out in either direction—any number of threads may be withdrawn to achieve the desired effect. To withdraw threads, gently lift them out with the needle to avoid distortion. Pull each thread out separately the entire length of the fabric or finish the corners. To finish corners (figure 2-30), snip each thread, leaving enough at the ends so that they can be rewoven into the fabric (1). Weave the needle into the corner, following the threads accurately. Pull snipped threads back into the fabric, staggering the ends. When the ends are embroidered, they will be nearly invisible (2).

2-30.

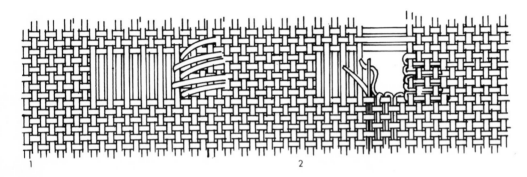

Basic Hemstitch

This stitch makes a beautiful finish for the edges of a wool scarf. Be sure all edges to be hemmed are straight and on-grain. Turn the hem (also turning in the raw edge one-quarter inch) up to the desired width; baste in place. Withdraw two or more threads just above the hem. To embroider, work from left to right. Reinsert the needle about two threads below the drawn area (through all thicknesses if you are hemming as well) to the outside. Pass the needle behind two or more threads at the opening edge. Take a stitch alongside the threads to be tied into a bundle, inserting the needle in the back and bringing it out two threads below (figure 2-31). Pull the thread taut to create the design.

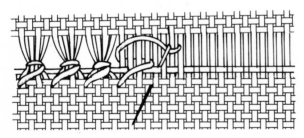

2-31.

Ladder Hemstitch

This stitch was used on the front of the white linen blouse shown on page 85. It can be done with or without a hem. Work one edge of the opening over two or more threads, using basic hemstitch embroidery. Turn the work and embroider along the remaining edge, tying the same threads in bundles (figure 2-32).

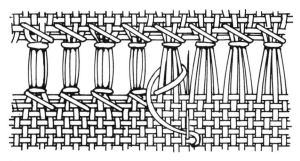

2-32.

Chevron Hemstitch

This stitch was used with a hem to create lovely bands of openwork in the fragment shown in figure 2-27. Using basic hemstitch embroidery, work along one edge, tying four or six threads together into a bundle. Turn the work and embroider along the remaining edge. Split the first bundle in half and secure. Continue over the same number of threads to form chevrons (figure 2-33).

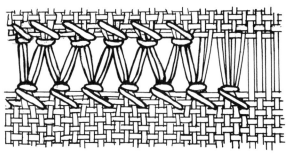

2-33.

Overcast Openwork

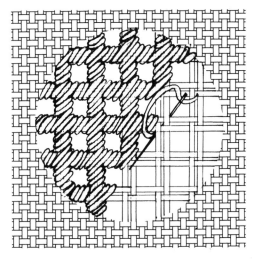

2-34.

This lovely latticework pattern is created by removing and retaining two threads alternately. Snip the same two threads at each edge of the design and remove them gently, starting with the crosswise threads and repeating the same procedure for the lengthwise threads. Start at the bottom and work diagonally to the top. Stitches should be close and firm. Overcast the threads diagonally (figure 2-34), working across one bar to the insertion and then up along the adjoining bar. Finish the outer edge with buttonhole stitch (figure 2-16).

Drawn Fabricwork

This technique is used to make openings in the fabric weave without breaking the threads. Threads are pulled quite taut in the hoop, creating holes and ridges that become more defined when the fabric relaxes. Use a blunt-pointed needle. You must be able to count each thread on the fabric. Stitches are graphed to show the correct spacing.

Buttonhole Flower

This simple design needs only a few guidelines on the fabric. Make a flower with four or five petals and fan the buttonhole stitches (figure 2-16) around each petal, radiating from the center hole (figure 2-35).

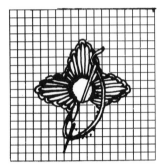

2-35.

Drawn Eyelet

The green silk yarn holder shown on page 81, signed "Rebekah Warren," was decorated with these simple drawn eyelets. The "sleeve" was designed to slip on the arm, and one side was divided into sections to separate the yarn and keep it within easy reach. A small flap was made to hold needles, with a gathered pouch to hold equipment. To make the eyelet, use the first version of the satin stitch (figure 2-12). Work over the threads on all four sides, with every stitch emerging from the same hole at the center. To form the hole, pull each stitch tightly as you work (figure 2-36).

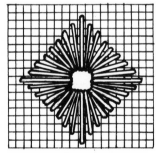

2-36.

44

Raised Diagonal Band

This pattern can be worked as a solid surface, in rows, or with other drawn stitches. At least two rows are needed to make lacy openings. The pattern is made by forming crosses over six or more threads. Bring the needle outside between threads, count up six threads, insert the needle, bring it out three threads to the left and three threads down, then insert it again six threads above. Complete a row of vertical stitches across the design in this manner. Work back over the vertical stitches, placing the long thread horizontally across them. Insert the needle in the same holes, pulling the stitches taut to make larger openings and ridges (figure 2-37).

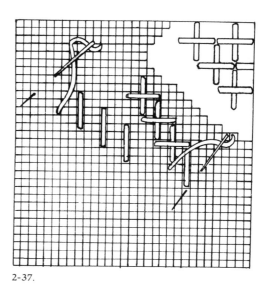

2-37.

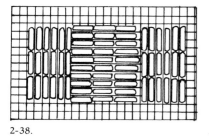

2-38.

Chessboard

This design forms blocks of three ridges, worked vertically and horizontally (figure 2-38). Use the first version of the satin stitch (figure 2-12), pulling each stitch tightly as you work.

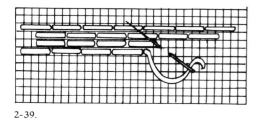

2-39.

Chained Border

This pattern can be worked either straight or diagonally; either in bands or as a solid surface. The stitches are worked over four threads—one side of the chain is worked first, then the other. On the top row bring the needle to the outside between threads, count over four threads, insert the needle, and bring it out two threads to the left and one thread down. Insert the needle four threads to the right and bring it out again at the end of the first stitch on the first row. Work over four threads, alternating between the two rows to the edge of the design and pulling threads tightly. On the bottom row reverse the procedure so the two center lines fall over the same four threads and in the same holes (figure 2-39). To work the chain diagonally, pass the stitches over four thread intersections.

Mosaic Diamond

This pattern is worked with a tightly drawn satin stitch, first version (figure 2-12), leaving a space of two threads between each row of diamonds. The diamond is shaped by working over two, four, six, eight, six, four, and two threads, respectively (figure 2-40). The next rows start with the longest stitch beneath the shortest stitch.

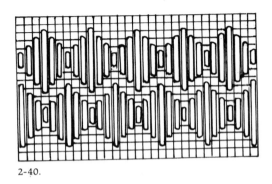

2-40.

Cutwork

In cutwork stitches are worked in a design around an area that is later cut away. There are many complex designs, but they were not practiced until the middle of the nineteenth century. The four simple stitches shown here were used in colonial embroidery.

Scalloped Buttonhole Border

As shown in the gauze muslin kerchief, (figure 2-29), the needleworkers' favorite—buttonhole stitch (figure 2-16)—serves yet another function. Work the stitch along the design (figure 2-41), leaving enough fabric outside the scallops so that a hoop can be used. When the design is completed, cut away excess fabric along the stitches, making sure that you do not cut into the embroidery!

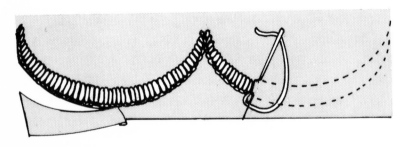

2-41.

46

Cut Eyelet

Trace a circle on the fabric and make a line of tiny running stitches around the circle (figure 2-42). Cut a cross across the circle towards the running stitches (1). Turn the cut edges under with the needle and overcast the edges with short, closely placed stitches (2). Smaller eyelets may be made by forming a hole with an awl and embroidering.

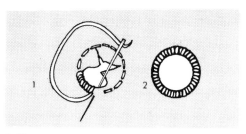

2-42.

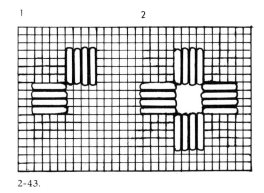

2-43.

Satin Block

These geometric openings (figure 2-43) were favored by colonial needleworkers because of their simplicity. They appear on the white handkerchief-linen blouse shown in page 85. Using the first version of the satin stitch (figure 2-12), start on the top row in the lower-right-hand corner and make four vertical stitches over four threads. Next, make four horizontal stitches over four threads, bringing out the first thread in the same hole (at the corner) that is used for the last vertical stitch (1). Complete the other two sides of the square in the same manner. Carefully cut out the fabric in the center (2).

Satin Eyelet

With the simple addition of four threads the satin block becomes an eyelet. Make it in the same way, adding a third stitch in the same hole used to form the corner and passing over four threads (figure 2-44).

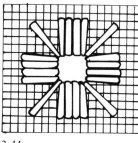

2-44.

Insertionwork

This lacy and very feminine type of embroidery stitch is sometimes called *faggoting*. Designs are embroidered between two separate fabric strips, thus serving as a bond. It has traditionally been used for delicate lingerie and household linens, and it surfaces again and again as a designer touch. Today, a machine-made counterpart is being used on dresses, blouses, and body shirts.

You are not limited to any particular type of fabric—just match the type and quality to the occasion. The lovely blue satin evening dress with silver lamé embroidery shown on page 84 is a perfect example of the versatility of this technique. Instructions for making this dress and other insertion-work garments is given in Chapter 5.

You will need a graph-paper gauge for these stitches. Cut a strip of two-inch-wide graph paper with one-eighth- to one-quarter-inch grids and tape together, matching gridlines. Edges to be embroidered must be narrow-hemmed or faced. To hem the edges, turn the raw edges in a scant three-eighths inch and pin, placing the pins on the outside of the panel. Turn in the folded edges three-eighths inch, pin, and baste.

To make openings, cut strips one and three-quarters inches wide to the desired length plus three-quarters inch. Cut the graph-paper strip to the same measurements. Pin the paper to the wrong side of the fabric strip. Place the strip on your material, with the right sides together (figure 2-45). Stitch a quarter-inch-wide rectangle to the planned length, pivoting at corner (1). Cut between the stitching to the end of the rectangle, clipping diagonally into the corners (2). Gently remove the paper. Turn the strip edges inside along the seam and press. Turn the raw edges inside three-eighths inch and baste (3). Sew short ends in place. Place the opening on top of the graph paper, keeping the edges one-quarter inch apart, and complete with the desired insertion stitches.

2-45.

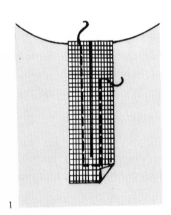
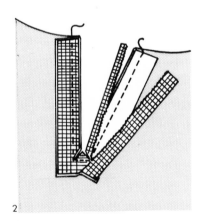
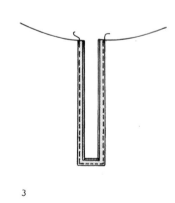

1   2   3

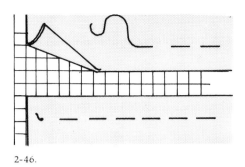
2-46.

After the edges are hemmed or faced, pin one section of the fabric over the graph paper, with the fold along a line near the center. Turn the work over and, with a contrasting color, baste along a graph-paper line one-quarter inch in from the fold (figure 2-46). This basting will serve as a guide for the stitch depth. Place the corresponding panel on the other side of the paper, leaving one-quarter inch between the two. (Wider or narrower openings can be made by adjusting the hem width.) Pin and baste in place, matching upper and lower edges and easing in any fullness evenly along the line.

Start any insertion stitch with a thread eighteen to twenty-four inches long. Knot the thread and hide it in the hem folds. To end a thread, fasten it securely on the inner hem fold. Start a new thread by bringing it out through the last knot (or purl) so the thread will be continuous. Keep your needle and stitches parallel to the grid lines and make the stitches one-quarter inch deep, sewing the hem in place as you embroider.

Knotted Buttonhole Insertion

This stitch is worked from left to right. To start, bring the thread out through the fold at the opening edge and make a stitch (figure 2-47). (Work stitches in groups of three, each one-eighth inch apart, with the center stitch three-eighths inch long.) Form a full circle with the thread, always keeping the thread under the point and eye of the needle (1). Pull the thread up to form a purl on the opening edge (2). Thread that is carried over the opening will have a twist but not a true purl. Simply hold it down with your thumbnail as you pull up the next stitch.

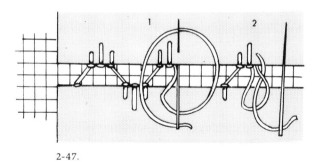
2-47.

Knotted Cretan Insertion

This stitch is worked from right to left. To start, insert the needle one-quarter inch from the edge of the fabric. Carry the thread across the opening. Insert the needle from the outside, with the thread underneath. Pull the thread out straight at the grid line, holding it taut with your thumb. Swing the thread in a half-circle, insert the needle under the crossed threads and over the loop, and pull the knot taut (figure 2-48).

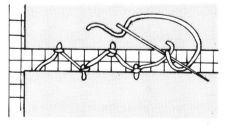
2-48.

Faggot Bundles

These stitches are worked from right to left. Make the first stitch a little slack. Bring the thread to the outside one-quarter inch from the opening edge. Take two stitches across the opening (figure 2-49). Swing the thread in a half-circle above or below. Insert the needle under the first two stitches and their carrying threads and then over the loop. Pull the thread to form a knot over the bundle. Pull the thread down straight and hold it with your thumb as you take a running stitch one-quarter inch from the edge to complete one bundle and start the next.

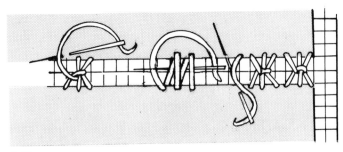

2-49.

Cretan Stitch

This stitch is worked from left to right. Insert the needle parallel to the grid lines and over the thread (figure 2-50). Narrow spaces are recommended.

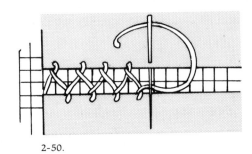

2-50.

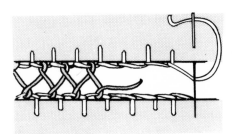

2-51.

Cretan-and-Blanket Stitch

Work blanket stitch (figure 2-53) along each edge, using the grid lines for spacing. With a second color of thread or yarn, work Cretan stitch on the top bars of blanket stitch (figure 2-51).

Reverse Romanian Stitch

Use a firm-textured thread to hold this stitch: limp threads may not stay in place. Make a vertical stitch over the opening. With the needle to the left of the stitch, insert it into the opposite edge—the thread will twist around the vertical stitch when it is pulled through (figure 2-52).

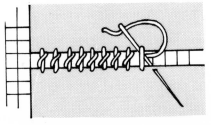

2-52.

Edgestitching

These lovely filigree helpmates perform two functions—they are visually attractive, and they hold a narrow hem in place. Any firmly made thread or yarn can be used. Simply match the quality to the wear the embroidered edge will receive.

Use a thread eighteen to twenty-four inches long. To start, hide the knot in the fold of the hem. To end, take the thread inside and fasten securely to the inner hem fold. To start a new thread, bring it out through a twist or knot of the last stitch so the thread will be continuous.

To help space the stitches evenly, simply pin a strip of graph paper under the edge of the fabric, with the fold along a grid line. From the paper side baste along a grid line one-quarter inch from the fold to make a depth gauge.

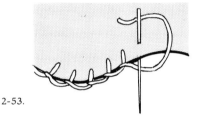

2-53.

Blanket Stitch

This stitch is worked from left to right. Bring the needle out through the hem edge. Insert it to the desired depth and bring it out over the thread, forming a loop. Draw the thread up so the stem is taut and the bar lies along the hem edge (figure 2-53). (The same procedure is used for crewel embroidery, with the thread passing outside along a design line instead of along the hem edge.)

Blanket-Stitch Variations

These lacy lovelies are just "twisted" versions of the same techniques. For the first (figure 2-54) form inverted Vs with the stem (1) or cross the stems to form Xs (2). Make a pair of blanket stitches, then form a knot over them by inserting the needle under the stems and over the loop (3).

The next variation (figure 2-55) has a knot and a scallop. Make a blanket stitch, forming a scallop with the bar (1). Form a half-circle to the right and insert the needle in the opposite direction along the first stem. Pull the thread down, forming a knot (2).

2-54.

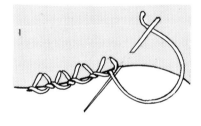

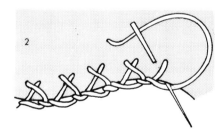

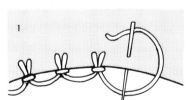

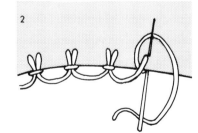

2-55.

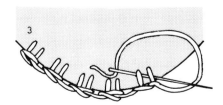

Knotted Blanket Stitch

This stitch is basically the same as the blanket stitch, but before pulling it taut, make a half-circle with the thread. Insert the needle under the crossed threads and over the loop and pull up, forming a knot (figure 2-56).

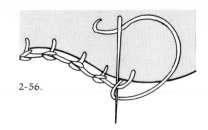

2-56.

Braid Stitch

Work from right to left, holding the edge away from you. Bring the needle out through hem edge and form a loop; insert the needle through the loop and the fabric (figure 2-57). Hold the loop down with your thumb as you pull the thread away from you. Tighten the knot to form neatly placed knots and scallops.

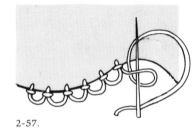

2-57.

Whitework

With the advent of prosperity in the eighteenth century, isolation and rugged conditions were no longer a daily problem in the colonies. Women had more time to pursue their needlework and to embellish it. Many of the French settlers were aristocrats who came to America to seek political refuge—the women brought with them their delicate whitework. Soon they were teaching others, sometimes setting up needlecraft schools. Since whitework is simply employing any embroidery technique using white fabric and white threads for the stitches, it allowed the craftswoman a choice between firm and pronounced or dainty and delicate bits of white finery for her home or for personal adornment.

Linen, muslin, and organdy were used for the foundation fabric in weights ranging from filmy transparents to heavyweight, textured homespuns. They were always embroidered with white threads of cotton, silk, wool, linen, or flax, whose twisted strands and plies could be as delicate or as bold as the worker desired.

The baby caps shown in figure 2-28 are examples of whitework utilizing different embroidery techniques. Both are summer caps; winter caps were heavily padded and often quilted. All baby clothes were adorned with a wide variety of needlework, as they were basically shapeless linen gowns drawn at the neck with a narrow tape.

Stumpwork

Stumpwork is embroidery with a raised surface or embroidery done over a padded surface. Other elements may also be included; bits of lace, feathers, beads, or other materials that will create a sculptural projection on the foundation. Unfortunately, most of the more elaborate examples of stumpwork shown in museums today are identified as English. Many of them have taken years to complete. The figures had painted, sometimes carved, faces with elaborate costumes worked over the stump, which was usually a piece of soft, shaped wood—hence the name "stumpwork." Strands of real hair were embroidered in place on the heads, and men's hats were completed with bits of felt and a tiny feather.

The earliest example of American stumpwork found so far is an embroidered picture illustrating the story of Queen Esther and Ahasuerus, worked by Rebekah Wheeler at the age of nineteen, signed, and dated 1664 on the back (figure 2-58). Miss Wheeler was the daughter of Lieutenant Joseph Wheeler, who was among the first group to settle in Concord, Massachusetts.

The picture shown on page 88 is a contemporary interpretation of stumpwork, which incorporates crewel-embroidery stitches as well. Chain stitch was used for the tree leaves and bushes; satin stitch, for the feet and bill of the chicks; brick stitch, to give a shaded effect to the sand; and French knots, for the cattails, with stem stitches to hold them up. Long and short running stitches were used for the grass blades, and outline stitch and split stitch for the fence. Craftsmen no longer use grasses and twigs for padding and stitches to give a bas-relief effect to the embroidery (although there is no reason why you cannot do so). One word of caution: since you *must* use a hoop, be sure to keep the stumpwork areas in mind. It's virtually impossible and most undesirable to move the hoop around too much.

2-58. Stumpwork picture, made by Rebekah Wheeler, signed and dated 1664 on the back. *Courtesy of the Concord Antiquarian Society.*

The stump is really a stuffed appliqué. While the classic cotton used for quilts is the best fabric to use, tricot knits work well too—more stuffing can be added without distorting the foundation fabric. To form the stump (figure 2-59), transfer the pattern to the right side of the fabric, including any design lines to be embroidered. Cut the patch, allowing a quarter-inch seam allowance (1). Turn the raw edges in along the outline, clipping the seam allowance as you fold so it will lie flat, and baste (2). Place the patch in position and pin. Slip-stitch the patch to the foundation (figure 3-18), leaving an opening for the stuffing. Don't break off the thread. Insert bits of cotton, using a scissors tip to slide them into position (3). Keep stuffing until a smooth surface is obtained without distorting the foundation fabric. Close the opening with slip-stitches. Embroider any design lines on top of the stump to accent body movement or dimension (4). Cover the stump with Ceylon, detached buttonhole, or darning stitches (figures 2-61, 2-62, and 2-63, respectively).

Figure 2-60 shows the design that was used to make the stumpwork picture shown on page 88. Ceylon stitch was worked very tight on the rabbit, and quite loose on the tree trunk and branches. Detached buttonhole stitch was worked quite tight, using a fuzzy yarn on both chicks. Darning stitch was used on the mushroom. Use this pattern to get the "feel" of stumpwork or create a design of your own, using the suggested stitches.

2-59.

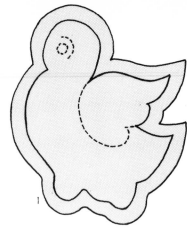

2-60.

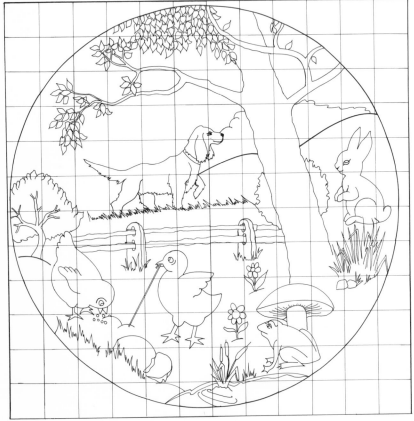

each square = 1 inch

54

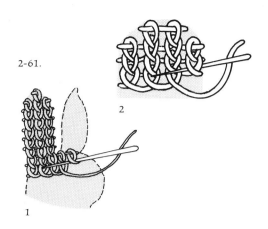

2-61.

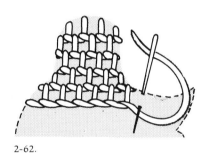

1

2

Ceylon Stitch

Use a blunt-pointed needle. This stitch is worked in rows that are detached across the design and anchored along the edges (figure 2-61). It was used to cover the rabbit in the stumpwork picture (1). Make it tight to look like knitting, or open for a lacy effect. Make a line of backstitches (figure 2-8) along the upper edge of the design for a foundation. Take the needle underneath to the left side at the end of each row. Working from left to right, insert the needle under the foundation stitch to form a loop and make a row of detached loops. Reinsert the needle on the left side and make another row of loops, this time inserting the needle under the crossed threads of the previous row (2). With a little practice you will be able to make uniform loops. You can add loops at the beginning and end threads of the previous row, where they emerge from the fabric. Decrease loops by anchoring the crossed threads with a tiny stitch. At the lower edge of the design, anchor all loose crossed threads in the same manner.

Detached Buttonhole Stitch

Use a blunt-pointed needle. Work rows of blanket stitch (figure 2-53), detached across the design and anchored along all edges. It can be as tight or as loose as desired. Make a line of backstitches (figure 2-8) at the upper edge of the design as a foundation. Take the needle underneath and to the left at the end of each row. Working from left to right, insert the needle under each foundation stitch and make a blanket stitch. Make a row of detached stitches. Reinsert the needle on the left side and make another row of blanket stitch, this time between each bar thread of the previous row (figure 2-62). With a little practice you will be able to make stitches of uniform length. Add stitches at each end of a row, over the thread where it emerges from the fabric. To decrease, anchor the bar with a tiny stitch. At the lower edge of the design, anchor all free bars in the same manner.

2-62.

Darning Stitch

Use both sharp- and blunt-pointed needles. This stitch is a simple exercise in weaving. With a sharp-pointed needle lay the vertical stitches over the design, taking tiny stitches at the top and bottom of the design with a sharp needle. With a blunt-pointed needle work from right to left, weaving the needle over and under the vertical threads without catching the fabric (figure 2-63). Insert the needle into the fabric at the left edge and return to the right edge. Repeat the weave, alternating the over-and-under procedure on the vertical threads as shown. Keep the threads taut in both directions.

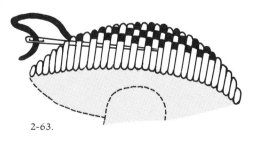

2-63.

Turkeywork Fabric Stitch

This pile stitch can be cut when you want a "fuzzy" surface to represent an animal's hair, or left in loops to look like a flower. Use a sharp-pointed needle. Work from the bottom of the design upward or start at the outer edge of a circle and work in. To begin, insert the needle from right to left under a thread or two of the foundation fabric. Pull the yarn through, leaving an end about half an inch long (figure 2-64). With the yarn above the stitch, insert the needle from right to left under the adjoining threads, coming out at the same hole where the first stitch was started (1). Pull the yarn to form a knot over the two stitches. Keeping the yarn below the needle, repeat this two-step knot, forming a quarter-inch loop between each knot. To end the yarn, clip to half an inch at the completion of a knot. Clip all loops to the same length (2). Stagger the stitches in each row to scatter the loops.

Couching Stitch

This stitch is used to form a raised outline. Use a sharp-pointed needle. Use thick, firm yarn or cord for the foundation thread—several strands of yarn or thread may be used, with a thinner thread or yarn for the anchoring stitch. To hide the ends of the foundation, bring the thread out through the fabric and lay it along the design lines, inserting it again at the end of the line. Holding the foundation taut, work from right to left. Bring the anchoring thread to the outside along the foundation. Take a stitch across the foundation to anchor it in place. Space the anchoring threads one-quarter to one-half inch apart along the foundation (figure 2-65).

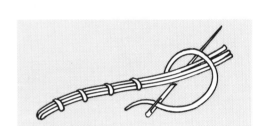

2-65.

Canvas Embroidery

Turkeywork

Turkeywork was an innovative canvas embroidery devised by colonial women in the seventeenth century. Beautiful Turkish carpet designs were simulated with whatever materials were available. Simple knot stitches were embroidered on a wide variety of fabrics, ranging from very fine handkerchief linen to heavy linsey-woolsey homespun. The colorful turkeywork settee shown on page 83 is covered with the original polychrome upholstery. The maple frame has hand-turned legs, with sausage turnings on the stretchers. It has a course hemp-canvas foundation that is visible where the nap has worn off from use. It was worked in 1675 in the Massachusetts colony. The handsome turkeywork side chair shown in figure 2-66 was sometimes called a "farthingale" chair because the seat was higher than normal and the low back was specifically designed for women wearing hooped skirts. Worked on the same type of hemp canvas, it was probably made in the Connecticut colony between 1650 and 1675. It has been repaired, but the original marsh-grass stuffing, spool, block-turned legs, and stretchers remain.

Turkeywork fell out of favor as the colonies prospered and Far Eastern carpets were imported by the well-to-do. But this mysterious and fascinating canvas embroidery certainly proves to be a marvelous conversation piece. The contemporary turkeywork handbag shown on page 85 is a testimonial to those beautiful home furnishings and bed rugs made by our foremothers. (Instructions for making the turkeywork handbag are found in Chapter 5.)

2-66. Turkeywork side chair. *Courtesy of the Metropolitan Museum of Art. Bequest of Mrs. J. Insley Blair, 1952.*

Turkeywork Canvas Stitch

This stitch is worked on penelope rug canvas, seven meshes to the inch, with three-ply Persian tapestry yarn and a blunt-pointed tapestry needle. Start at the lower-left-hand corner of your design and work from left to right only, as the knots and the pile are closely placed. It is impossible to see the knotted foundation after the pile is clipped. Each knot stitch is worked around two threads, with the threads beginning and ending in the same opening (figure 2-67). The pile can be as short as one-eighth inch or as deep as half an inch, depending on the yarn and canvas mesh used. The pile is sometimes left uncut, especially in stumpwork, when a raised-loop effect adds another dimension. To test the length of the pile, use the first or second mesh below the row as a loop gauge. For subsequent rows use the previous row as a gauge. Clip each row when it is completed.

To begin the stitch (figure 2-68), insert the needle from right to left under a thread; pull the yarn through, making the end about half an inch long (1). With the yarn above the stitch, insert the needle from right to left under the companion thread, forming a knot (2). Repeat this two-step knot over each set of double threads of the canvas, forming a loop of the desired pile depth between each knot. Keep the yarn *below* the needle for step (1), and *above* the needle for step (2). When you run out of yarn or if you want to change colors, be sure to complete both steps before starting another strand or color, clipping the yarn end even with the loops. When a row is completed, clip the loops, trimming the pile evenly if necessary (3).

2-67.

2-68.

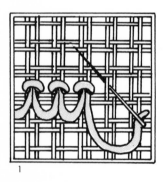  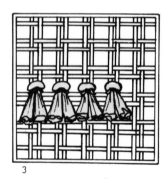

1   2   3

Whipstitch

Use this stitch for edges. Finish the exposed canvas edges. To start, insert the needle through the top of the fold from left to right and bring it out through a mesh close to the turkeywork. Pull the thread until only one inch remains in the fold. Next, insert the needle close to the lining from back to front under the two sets of double threads, forming a whipstitch over the folded canvas (figure 2-69). The canvas should be completely covered on both turkeywork and lining (or underside) sides as you work. Insert the needle from back to front on an angle through the next set of double threads or meshes all around the edges. End the yarn by running it under the stitches.

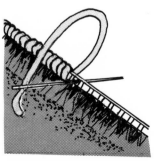

2-69.

Bargello

Canvas needlework continued to be a favorite of colonial women as their rough-hewn cabins expanded into comfortable farmhouses or modest village dwellings. So many canvas-needlework designs are readily available that I have chosen to emphasize the lesser-known examples of early American needlework. Some of them are so beautiful, however, that to ignore them completely would be a disservice. The elegant flame-stitched bargello pocketbook shown on page 82 could not be overlooked. The instructions in Chapter 5 will help you make a nearly exact duplicate.

Flame-Stitch

Use a blunt-pointed tapestry needle. Each stitch is worked over four canvas threads, and the needle is inserted under two threads to start the next stitch. These stitches can be worked either from right to left or from left to right, moving diagonally up or down over two threads (figure 2-70). To begin, bring the needle through a mesh to the outside, leaving about one inch on the underside. To hold the yarn end in place, work four or five stitches over it. To end a yarn, insert the needle to the underside and work it under four or five stitches on the back. Always cut your yarn off to change colors. Do not pull the yarn too tight.

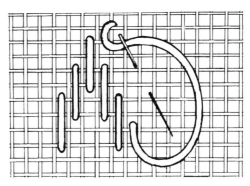

2-70.

Chapter 3

Innovative Bed Covers for Today

Bed covers were called by many names in colonial days, but none was more confusing than the terms used for "show" covers. Remember that these stalwart women did not make anything beautiful that was not practical as well: there was no room in their world for a pretty covering that had only to look good and enhance the room setting, as our bedspreads of today do. In the seventeenth and eighteenth centuries bedspreads with a foundation of heavy, coarse, natural- or bleached-wool fabric woven with thick wool threads were called "bed rugs." Since looms were narrow, the foundation was made of several strips of this heavy fabric in various styles to please the maker. These strips were sewn together with flat-fell or French seams, and the edges had hems about half an inch wide. Colonial bed rugs were adorned with richly colored wool yarns. Many were covered with luxurious loop pile, clipped turkeywork yarns, or handsome embroidered designs.

The bed rug shown on page 82 was embroidered in loop-pile stitch by Mary Avery in 1722. It had open corners to fit around the bed posters, thus allowing the sides and ends to be longer for more warmth. The embroidered bed rug shown in figure 3-1 had rounded corners and did not extend over the edges of the bed as far. This gorgeous bed rug is lighter in weight, as the foundation of linsey-woolsey is not completely covered. The Deerfield blue embroidery design reflects the Far Eastern influence so popular with needlecrafters in the eighteenth century. The border has two basic flowers and sprays, with a bunch of grapes in each scallop. Notice how each one has been embroidered with a different pattern. The border is decorated with indigo blue wool crewel-embroidery yarn, accented with pale blue wool yarn, and finished off with a fringe.

Any lightweight bed cover, coverlet, or quilt was called a "counterpane." It was warm enough to keep the family warm on a chilly spring night, but the lighter fabric allowed the ardent home crafter more freedom in technique, such as a white-on-white quilt with elaborate stuffed designs or a homespun fabric embroidered with candlewicking or crewel.

Most counterpanes had a light- to medium-weight foundation, such as dimity, bleached muslin, linen, or a twill-weave cotton. Others were quilted, using white fabric with thin wadding between the layers to make a lighter-weight quilt.

3-1. Wool Deerfield blue bed rug, made in Connecticut, eighteenth century. *Courtesy of the Brooklyn Museum.*

"Comforter" was the name given to thick, lightweight bed covers with a puffy surface—they are now enjoying a revival as a utilitarian show cover. A comforter was made of two layers of fabric sewn together, stuffed for warmth—with a wide variety of materials ranging from grass to unspun wool—and knotted at even intervals to keep the filling from shifting.

Quilts were and still are the classic bedspread. Pioneer women brought beautifully quilted bed covers with them to America. As time took its toll on these prized possessions, it was necessary to mend them. Unfortunately, it was impossible to match the original fabric exactly, so colonial women started to patch their quilts with any available fabric, and soon they were creating completely new-looking bed covers. Making quilts "from scratch" soon occurred to some ingenious craftswoman. Using every available scrap of fabric, new and used, a new art form was developed—patchwork quilts.

There are so many possibilities available when the secrets of these fantastic bed covers are unlocked. If you would like to embroider a priceless, one-of-a-kind bedspread, the instructions in this chapter will start you on your way. If a bed rug seems overwhelming, you can try out any of these embroidery techniques on smaller projects first, such as the pocketbook or the skirt described in Chapter 5.

Bed Rugs

These beautiful bed coverings were inspired by carpets from India, so it's not so surprising that they continued to be called "rugs" even though they were used on a bed. Since canvas was not available at first to colonial women, they substituted their own homespun-wool fabric, which made a softer, less rigid bed cover. Bed rugs were considered valuable possessions and were often listed in account of estate settlements.

Loop-Pile Embroidery

The bed rug shown on page 82 was worked in loop-pile stitch with four-ply yarn. The heavy foundation was embroidered so carefully that very few stitches showed on the reverse side. This technique was easy for colonial women—they used a smooth stick or quill as a gauge to form precise circular loops and an adaptation of the simple running stitch. This almost forgotten embroidery stitch is an uncomplicated procedure. Wool yarns are a good choice for the embroidery, but knitting worsted and Persian tapestry yarn also make beautiful standing loops. These modern natural fibers work just as well as those used by the colonial women.

To make a loop-pile-stitch design, you will need a padded frame and T-pins (this will enable you to hold the fabric taut without crushing the loops), chenille needles and wool yarn, a round object for a gauge (a round pencil about three-eighths inch in diameter makes a beautiful loop), and a coarsely woven homespun-type cotton or wool foundation fabric. Rest the frame on a table or stand or between two chair backs so you can use both hands. Test your yarn and fabric before starting to stitch.

Loop-Pile Stitch

To start the stitch (figure 3-2), knot the yarn end and take a tiny stitch under a design line (1). Take another stitch alongside the first stitch, forming a loop over the gauge (2). Repeat this stitch along the design line, adjusting the space between the stitches so the loops stand up straight without fanning. End your yarn by taking several flat running stitches. These will be covered by loop stitches, and it will be hard to find the knots when your needlework is completed. This stitch is easy to master, and after two or three you'll be working the design. Work the loop-pile stitch along each design outline first and then fill it in. When you work the background, swirl the rows of loops for a richer look. They lose some of their charm if each row is lined up too evenly.

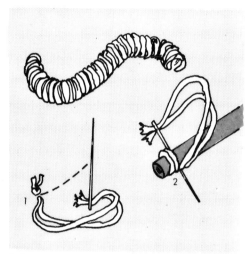

3-2.

Turkeywork

This form of embroidery was used by some colonial women to make bed rugs. On a heavy, loosely woven wool foundation fabric it made an extremely useful bed cover—the colonists learned early that several layers kept them warmer, and turkeywork bed rugs had three layers. The lower layer was the wool foundation; the middle layer consisted of closely placed knots of wool yarn; and the outer layer was clipped pile one-eighth to one-quarter inch deep.

To make turkeywork on a soft foundation such as the loosely woven linsey-woolsey those illustrious women used, the stitch should be made over two lengthwise threads. The stitch shown in figure 2-68 is for rug canvas, but you can use it on any type of canvas or loosely woven fabric. A padded frame with T-pins must be used, however, or the foundation will be pulled out of shape. A finer foundation can also be worked, and you don't have to count threads: use the turkeywork fabric stitch shown in figure 2-64.

Counterpanes

Many counterpanes were adorned with embroidery, and the most unusual type of embroidery was candlewicking. Innovative colonial women may have seen these beautiful spreads in England before coming to America—or perhaps a well-situated villager was able to import one—but, however they learned about them, needlewomen soon began making their own. The name "candlewicking" was given to this beautiful embroidery because the characteristic multiple-ply cordlike cotton yarn was originally used for candlewicks. A lovely combination of tufted and raised stitches was worked with this yarn, and much of the embroidery was done in white on a white foundation. The fantastic all-white candlewick-embroidered counterpane shown in figure 3-3 was made with a foundation of three strips of soft twill sewn together. The pineapple-and-floral composition shows a Far Eastern influence in its ruglike designs. The fringe around the sides and at the end was made in knotted buttonhole edgestitch, with scallops formed over a gauge for uniformity. The tassels were attached by folding several strips of thread in half to form a loop over the last row of scallops. The ends were then pulled through the loop, forming a knot at the center of the scallop.

Great care was taken by colonial needleworkers in transferring the designs to the white fabric. Each stitch was indicated by a dot, and these marks had to wash out easily. By coloring powdered laundry starch with liquid bluing and using a fine, stiff brush, embroiderers were able to transfer the pattern with a stencil. A stencil was made for one-fourth of the foundation by drawing in the design and then punching holes with an awl at half-inch or one-inch intervals. The stencil was sometimes made more durable by rubbing it with boiled linseed oil before punching the holes. The fabric was stretched on the floor or in a quilt frame before it was marked.

Straight-line borders were made by "snapping the string"—the same procedure used by carpenters. The string was rubbed with blued laundry starch, which was allowed to dry into a powder. Then the string was held taut by two people and pulled up, allowing it to snap against the fabric and leave a blue line. Today, you can buy blue carpenters' chalk that serves the same purpose, and it brushes off with little effort.

To do candlewicking embroidery, you will need a padded frame and T-pins. Small items can be embroidered on a stretcher frame as large as the item. The fabric must be kept taut, or it will pucker. Hoops are not advisable—they may not fit over the tufts and will certainly crush them. If you don't have a freestanding frame, rest your frame on a table or stand, since you need both hands to work. Blunt tapestry or yarn needles with large, long eyes are used.

The foundation fabric can be any cotton or linen fabric that has *not* been sanforized or preshrunk. Permanent-press or bonded fabrics will not work. The secret of this procedure is the foundation: when the embroidery is completed, dip the fabric in cold water to shrink; it will tighten around the yarn and hold it securely in place. After the cold-water bath shake out the excess water and brush the tufts gently, if needed, when they are dry.

I have successfully used all kinds of yarn for the embroidery—crochet and knitting cottons, rug yarns, synthetics, and every weight and ply of knitting wool—each had its own buoyancy, and the choice is yours. Before starting a project, determine how many strands each tuft will require: twelve or more strands will be needed, depending on the number of plies and the weight of the fibers of your selected yarn or thread. Some of the

3-3. Candlewick counterpane. *Courtesy of the Smithsonian Institution.*

cottons needed as many as twenty-four strands to make a nice, fluffy tuft. Make sure to get a yarn that matches your fabric. Don't be discouraged if you can't find it the first time around—don't compromise and ruin the effect. Make your own decision and don't be hassled by salespeople—you are the only person who can visualize the finished project.

Candlewick Running Stitch

This stitch requires four or more strands of thread. To make the stitch, bring the thread to the right side of the fabric. Take one-eighth-inch stitches along the design outline (or under the dots if you are using the colonial technique), leaving quarter- to half-inch spaces between them. Form a raised stitch over a gauge—use a crochet hook or a smooth stick (figure 3-4). It is also possible to lift up these stitches with the eye end of your needle as you work. Practice a few inches before starting a project. If you are working with four strands of yarn, it may be necessary at times to pull the yarn flat to keep it from twisting before raising the stitches.

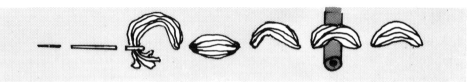

3-4.

Candlewick Tuft Stitch

Using two, four, or more strands of yarn, follow your design dots (spaced at one-inch intervals) with running stitches. Take a small stitch under each dot, return to each dot in turn, inserting the needle in the same holes until you have used half of the threads needed to make the desired tuft (figure 3-5). Then take more stitches at a right angle to the previous ones, using the same number of threads. Hold on to any loose thread ends as you stitch over the first stitches so the ends won't knot as you pull the thread through. Cut the threads at the center, fluff, and trim to a rounded form if necessary.

3-5.

Comforters

These simply made bed covers were a godsend to the busy colonial woman—a plain sheath of fabric, usually recycled, and some unusual materials were sufficient to keep her family warm. Common stuffing materials were grass, straw, cornhusks, rags, and feathers. These prudent women carefully collected every feather from a fowl used for food or gathered soft dried grass or even moss to replace the filling in a comforter for another winter. Dried materials like grass, straw, or cornhusks became very brittle and powdery from a winter's use.

You can recycle your faded, worn blankets: use them as batting for a comforter and give them new life—they never become lumpy. Use two lightweight blankets for extra warmth. Remove all binding and simply trim them to the desired size.

With the invention of polyester batting, these easy-to-make comforters have made a fantastic comeback. Cotton batting had a tendency to lump and could not be washed successfully. The cost of goose feathers made down comforters a luxury item.

You don't need a frame to make a comforter—just a large, flat surface. The comforter can be as luxurious or as inexpensive as your budget allows: use cotton flannel, calico, polished cotton, or some glamorous fabric— velveteen, silk, satin, velvet, corduroy, or wool. Some tightly knitted fabrics would make a beautiful comforter, and knits come in wide widths that require little piecing. One of the most serviceable and easiest to use is a pair of beautiful sheets—they are being used for everything today. You could decorate an entire bedroom with them, with your handsome new comforter as the focal point. For those of you who like to make quilt blocks—patchwork, appliqué, or embroidered squares—but are frightened at the thought of quilting an entire bedspread, a comforter is the perfect solution.

Size

Plan on a ninety-inch-long comforter for any bed. A width of about seventy inches is good for a twin bed, and about eighty inches for a double bed. Adapt these measurements to your needs—bunk-, queen-, and king-size beds have particular measurements—or make your comforter bedspread size. A bedspread will usually touch the floor on both sides and at the foot end, so measure across the bed (with bedding) and down each side to the floor for the width. Since this type of bed cover is fluffy, you may not want it to cover the pillows, but do take this into account when measuring the length of the bed and down the end to the floor.

Materials

You will need top and back fabric in the desired measurements, polyester batting or an old blanket in the same size (two layers make a fluffy, warm comforter), thread for sewing seams, durable thread or yarn for knotting T-pins, and large-eyed, long darning needles.

Assembly

Pin the two pieces of fabric with the right sides facing each other. Stitch the sides and one end, starting and ending six inches from the corners on the other end, using a half-inch seam allowance (figure 3-6).

Working on a flat surface, spread both layers out smoothly, with the back side on top (do not turn the right sides out). If you are using *batting*, place it over the fabric, inside the seam stitching, keeping all three layers smooth. If piecing is necessary, lap the edges about one inch and sew in place with extralong, loose running stitches. If you are using a *blanket*, prepare the three layers in the same manner. Pin either filling to the back of the fabric along the outer edges with T-pins, taking care not to catch the top (figure 3-7).

Carefully turn the comforter sheath right side out and transfer the pins to the right side, holding the batting in place. Smooth out the three layers on a flat surface and pin together; add more T-pins if necesary. Turn in the remaining raw edges half an inch and slip-stitch them together, keeping the comforter as flat as possible (figure 3-8). To start, bring the needle to the outside from the top fold. Take a tiny stitch (a thread or two) in the lower fold. Insert the needle through the top fold alongside the thread, taking a quarter-inch stitch. Swing the needle down to take a stitch in the lower fold. Repeat this process until the opening is sewn shut. To end, fasten the thread securely by taking three tiny stitches in the same spot.

The next step is to knot the batting in place. Starting at the outer edges, make knots six inches in from the edge, or along the seam of the border, at four- to six-inch intervals. If you are working on the floor, carefully slide the comforter over your legs to make the knots. As you move toward the center of an *undecorated* fabric or sheet, make the knots at twelve-inch intervals, with one knot in the center of each square formed by the knots. For *quilt* blocks, place a knot at each corner of the square and in the center.

3-6.

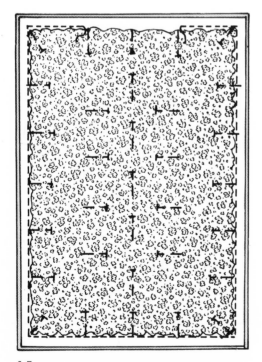

3-7.

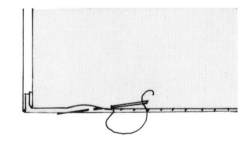

3-8.

Knot Stitch

Thread a large-eyed, sharp-pointed needle with about fifty inches of yarn and double it. Insert the needle down through all three layers, one-eighth inch away from the corner or mark, and bring it back up through all layers, one-eighth inch on the other side of the corner or mark, using a quarter-inch stitch (figure 3-9). Pull the yarn through, leaving a tail about two inches long (1). Tie the two strands into a square knot (2) and pull it together tightly (3). Cut the yarn off after the knot is tied, leaving about an inch. Repeat this simple procedure, adjusting the thread length to your needs.

3-9.

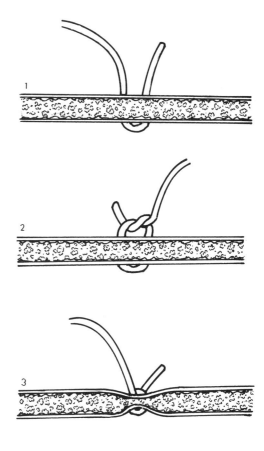

Handsewn Method

If you do not have a sewing machine, or if you prefer handsewn bed covers, comforters can be made entirely by hand. On a flat surface place the back wrong side up. Now place the batting or blanket on top and smooth both layers. Place the top over the batting right side up. Pin all three layers together with T-pins and baste if desired. Turn in all edges half an inch and slip-stitch them together as explained above. Knot the three layers together as instructed in figure 3-8.

To set a comforter in a quilt frame for knotting, follow the same procedure as for quilts, using the manufacturer's instructions. Then finish the edges with self-binding or bias binding (figure 3-20).

Quilts

Quilting is not only an American tradition: this needlecraft may have started in China or Egypt a thousand years before the birth of Christ. At some point in time the technique of sewing several layers of fabric and fibers together for additional warmth was invented. The Egyptians and Chinese wove luxurious fabrics, often with silver and gold threads, so quilting may have been invented as a means to glamorize fabric as well. Europeans expanded the quilting horizon with their beautiful silk and satin ecclesiastical robes, embellished with golden threads, and their royalty slept under quilted silk bed covers intricately stitched into elaborate designs. Some may have been appliquéd or embroidered, but none were made entirely of patchwork—this is a uniquely American craft, born of necessity.

When the quilts that the early settlers brought with them became worn, they were carefully mended by loving hands to retain their beauty. These patched quilts soon inspired some creative mind with the idea of making new bedcovers with recycled material. Every scrap of fabric was used and reused, and then the worn rags were sewn together in layers for batting— sometimes newspapers were used for the same purpose. The cold, hard winters made increasing demands on the ingenuity of these hardy women, and they quickly learned how to manage with the supplies at hand.

The first patchwork quilts were quite utilitarian, not the beautifully coordinated works of art that were made later. There was never enough fabric of one type, and the patterns were simple. Basic shapes—squares, rectangles, triangles—were used to make quilt tops, and often the colors were not vivid: recycled fabrics were partially washed-out or sun-faded.

As the colonists' situation improved, more fabric became available, either through their own resources or imported, so the colonial woman spent her winters piecing quilt blocks and assembling quilt tops. This home craft was usually done close to the fireplace in winter, since central heating was unheard of at that time. But when spring arrived, the home became a place for entertaining—friends were invited to help with the quilting, and the hostess spent days preparing food specialties. The guests rose early so the festivities could start; usually by eleven A.M. they were ready for the noon meal.

These ladies enjoyed themselves every minute. Gossip was exchanged, and each woman was able to bring her friends up-to-date on new arrivals and her own winter accomplishments as her fingers worked quickly and accurately. By sundown the ladies were joined by the menfolk and children for an evening meal that was talked about for days. Some of these quilting bees ended with games or a country dance. Each family looked forward to its turn to have another gala quilting bee.

Little girls were taught to piece quilts along with other needlecrafts. As they grew older, they became more accomplished, and by the time a girl was in her teens she could make beautiful quilt tops. Many of these became hope-chest items. A quilting bee was often the occasion to announce the engagement of a daughter—the townswomen came to help transform her first quilt top into a bed cover.

A lot of love and family history could be worked into a patchwork quilt. Favorite garments were often passed down or restyled for another member of the family, and, when the garment was no longer usable, the "good" sections were used to fashion quilt blocks. Even when fabric became easier to acquire, the women did not discard this new-found home craft. More elaborate designs were conceived, and patches of favorite garments, such as a birthday or party dress, were used. In the early nineteenth century autograph quilts were popular gifts for a friend who was moving to another town or for a well-liked pastor's wife.

The autograph presentation quilt shown in figure 3-10 was handmade of bleached muslin appliquéd with brightly colored cotton prints. There are sixty-one squares, and in the large center square an entire poem was written in longhand with indelible ink. Each of the smaller squares was done by a different person and bears the autograph of the worker. The squares were made, joined, lined, and quilted by the ladies of a Presbyterian church at Maltaville, New York, and the quilt was a gift to the pastor's wife, Mary Benton Barnard Hall, in April, 1847.

Practically every block in this quilt is different. If you have trouble deciding on a pattern to start your first appliqué quilt, don't hesitate to use one of these—craftswomen considered it an honor if their patches were copied, and these ladies would certainly be pleased for their designs to be perpetuated nearly one hundred and thirty years later.

Why not start an autograph quilt yourself and call on each of your friends and family to do a block for you? Supply each with a square of fabric and some scraps in your favorite color and ask each to autograph the completed square. It will give you and them everlasting pleasure.

The child's fruit-basket quilt shown in figure 3-11 was made in four cotton panels, using three shades of green, two of red, and a dark purple. The crab apples, cherries, strawberries, and grapes were stuffed, and chain stitch was used to embroider the fruit stems and most of the baskets. The handsome muslin curtain shown on page 85 has an appliquéd valance that was inspired by this beautiful quilt. (Directions for making the curtain are found in Chapter 5.)

3-10. Autographed presentation quilt. *Courtesy of the Smithsonian Institution.*

71

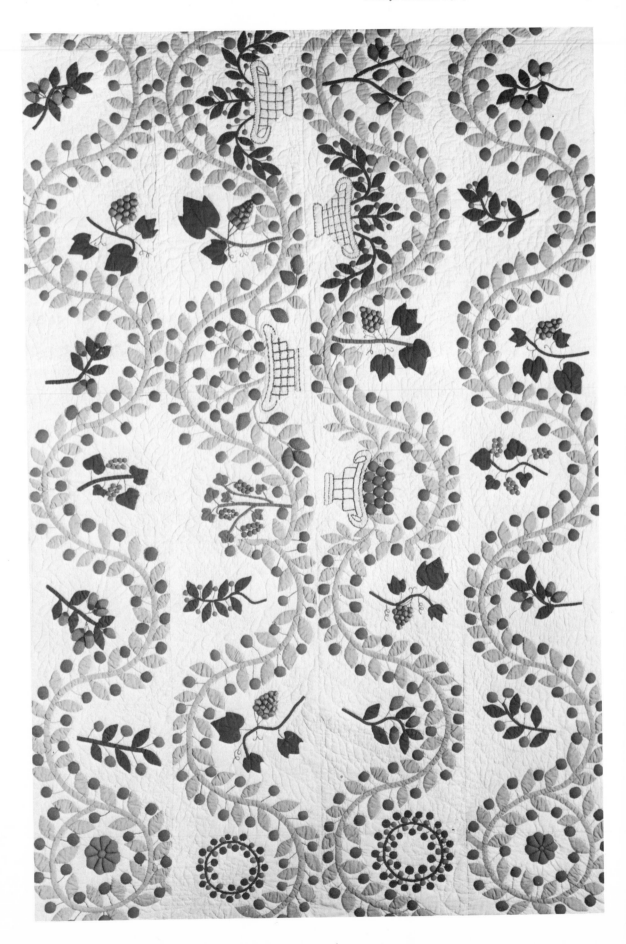

The Penn Treaty quilt shown in figure 3-12 was pieced by Martha Washington. It is a beautiful example of the use of simple geometrics to form an unusual quilt top. The center block is a copperplate textile depicting William Penn signing a treaty with the Indians. Moving outward from the center are a small outline of triangles and squares; a narrow, striped border with contrasting corner squares; an intriguing arrowhead band with evening-star corners; another narrow, striped border with contrasting corners; a band composed of larger squares and triangles with larger evening stars in each corner; a slightly wider border with corners of contrasting rectangles and squares; a band with five pinwheel blocks on each side and corners of four contrasting squares of the scenic printed fabric used in the center; and an outer border made of a wide strip of calico with contrasting corners.

3-12. Penn Treaty quilt made by Martha Washington. *Courtesy of the Mount Vernon Ladies' Association. Photo: Marler.*

The simple but elegant white cotton quilt shown in figure 3-13 is on display in the Blue Room at Mount Vernon. The pillow and the side and end panels are appliquéd with printed-fabric garlands of pink flowers with blue ribbons. The diamond patchwork around the edge of the bed has a center square appliquéd with a floral motif as well as an appliquéd border of striped fabric. The central section on top of the bed is composed of large blocks, some of which are also appliquéd. The fringe is made of netting. This outstanding example of early quilting combined both types of quilt-block techniques—patchwork and appliqué. The home crafter cut out designs from beautifully printed fabric instead of making her own. This unusually charming procedure should certainly set your mind to work. You don't need to create your own patches—simply select a beautiful printed fabric and use its designs for your appliqué.

There are many ways to construct a quilt, and the equipment can be elaborate or practically nonexistent. If you are just beginning this lovely, relaxing home craft, start out with small items such as potholders, place mats, pillows, or a purse and work up to making a quilt "from scratch." (Instructions for using quilting techniques to make a small purse are found in Chapter 5.) Try both appliqué and patchwork—see which technique is best suited to your personality. Does laying on intricate designs soothe your fraying nerves, or would you rather seam an array of geometric designs? Whatever your choice, it should be just right for you.

3-13. Appliqué and patchwork quilt. *Courtesy of the Mount Vernon Ladies' Association. Photo: Marler.*

There is also an almost infinite number of quilt patterns available. Figure 3-10 gives you over fifty different patterns to choose from. Figure 3-12 has beautiful examples of squares, rectangles, and triangles. The distinctive glazed-wool counterpane shown on page 83 is another example of the creative imagination of colonial women. Plain linsey-woolsey was made glamorous by glazing the fabric with a hot, flat iron—a procedure any dressmaker avoids at all costs—and then transforming it into a quilted bed cover imposing enough to please the most discriminating person.

Select your quilt-block design from these illustrations or one of the many other sources. It can be any size or shape. It can be a design made up of small patches inside a square or rectangle, or a one-patch design such as the hexagons, honeycombs, and diamonds used to make allover patterns. Some more simplified designs are shown in figure 3-14.

Quilt-Block Pattern

Work out your pattern on graph paper, taping several sheets together for larger quilt blocks. Patchwork designs are often divided into four, eight, nine, or sixteen smaller squares, and you may not have to draw the entire block. Appliqué blocks may need some dividing lines to enable you to place the patches correctly.

3-14.

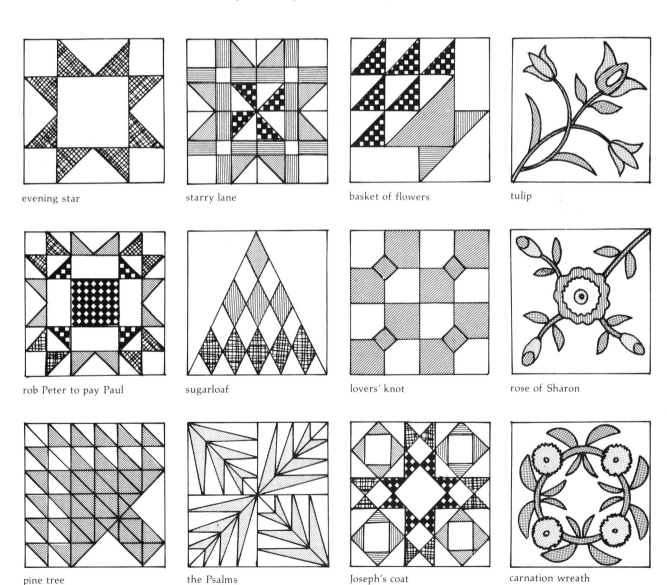

evening star

starry lane

basket of flowers

tulip

rob Peter to pay Paul

sugarloaf

lovers' knot

rose of Sharon

pine tree

the Psalms

Joseph's coat

carnation wreath

Make individual pattern pieces. This is a very important step—the patches will not fit properly if the pieces are not made accurately. Carefully trace each design shape, using tracing paper. If you plan to sew your patchwork-quilt blocks together by machine, add a one-quarter-inch seam allowance on all pattern edges. Make permanent, durable patterns from heavy cardboard, sandpaper, or clear plastic (buy this at an art store or recycle an empty bleach container—it flattens quite easily).

Yardage

Now that you have decided on a pattern, the next step is to make a small diagram of the quilt. Take into consideration the distance from the top of the bed to the floor, whether you plan to have a dust ruffle, and whether the quilt will cover the pillows (add an extra eighteen or twenty inches for this). The most important factor is *shrinkage*—the quilting process compresses the fabric as it is worked, so always allow four to eight inches extra for this or you will have a smaller quilt than planned.

A quilt-top layout will help you judge the fabric more accurately (figure 3-15). To make a top seventy-two by eighty-eight inches with quilt blocks, contrasting strips, and borders (1), you will need twenty twelve-and-one-half-inch squares, fifteen strips four and one-quarter by twelve and one-half inches, four strips four and one-half by sixty and one-half inches, two strips six and one-half by seventy-six and one-half inches, two strips six and one-half by sixty and one-half inches, and four corner squares six and one-half by six and one-half inches.

To make a top seventy-two by ninety-six inches with quilt blocks and a patchwork border (2), you will need eighteen decorative twelve-and-one-half-inch squares, seventeen contrasting squares the same size, two patchwork strips six and one-half by eighty-four and one-half inches, two patchwork strips six and one-half by sixty and one-half inches, and four corner squares six and one-half by six and one-half inches.

To make a quilt top with diagonal blocks (3) or with diagonal patchwork (4), adapt the strips to add the additional width and length needed beyond the blocks, remembering that both the blocks and the strips must have a quarter-inch seam allowance on all edges.

To estimate the yardage for a quilt top, multiply the number of blocks you have for each color and make a diagram for each pattern piece for each color. Trace as many pattern pieces as you can on a nine-by-twenty-two-inch piece of paper (fabric stores won't sell less than a quarter yard), trying not to waste space; allow half an inch between pattern pieces, placing them straight and on-grain. For contrasting strips and borders make a minilayout so you can estimate their yardage more accurately.

To estimate the yardage for the quilt back, you will need to take the binding into account (figure 3-20). Since the back is made from one piece of fabric (five to seven yards long), do not seam down the center of it—this may distort the center of the quilt top. Use a whole width at the center, with two narrower strips on each side. Most cottons measure forty-four or forty-five inches in width. Sheets may also be used to advantage, especially for quilt backs, borders, and contrasting strips. Be sure to allow a quarter-inch seam allowance when you piece fabric strips together. The back should be at least one and one-half inches larger all around than the top.

3-15.

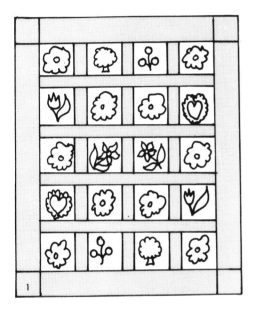

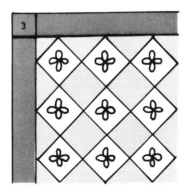

Blocks

Now that you have made all the preliminary plans and purchased the supplies, you are ready to really get started on your quilt. Whether you are doing patchwork, appliqué, or both, cutting out the patches is the first step. For appliqués, also cut the foundations in the desired size carefully on the straight grain.

Accuracy in marking and cutting is the byword here—use a dark-colored pencil for light fabrics and a lighter one for dark fabrics. To mark the patterns (figure 3-16), trace *patchwork* on the wrong side of the fabric (1), and *appliqué* on the right side of the fabric (2), allowing half an inch between each pattern. Be sure to place the patterns on the straight grain. Cut out each patch, using a quarter-inch seam allowance.

3-16.

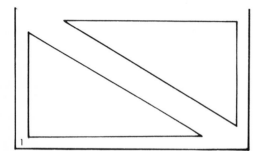 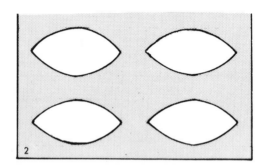

If the design calls for *bias strips*—for stems, etc.—cut the strip twice the width of the pattern. The two edges of the fabric must be on the straight grain: cut along a thread to straighten the edge. Fold down the corner at a forty-five-degree angle, then cut along the fold (figure 3-17). Mark the strips and cut them apart, cutting along the length grain to form a slanted end (1). Join the slanted ends (2), piecing as often as needed, and press the seams open (3).

For appliqué bias strips, turn them in until the edges meet at the center and press. If the bias is to be curved, form it into shape by stretching one folded edge slightly as you press it, making sure not to distort the width.

To make a *patchwork* block, place two patches right sides together and match the outlines. Sew along one line at a time with tiny running stitches, starting with a knot and ending with several tiny backstitches. When the entire block is joined, press the seam allowances to one side. Excess bulk at corners may be trimmed if necessary. To make an *appliqué* block, turn in the edges along the outline and baste. Position bias strips on the block before other patches, such as leaves or flowers. Baste bias strips and patches in place before sewing permanently.

3-17.

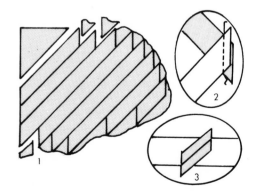

Slip-stitch

All appliqués should be slip-stitched in place (figure 3-18). Bring the thread to the outside, catching a thread or two of the appliqué. Directly below the thread take a scant quarter-inch stitch in the block and swing the needle up to catch a thread or two of the appliqué. Repeat this procedure, adjusting the length of the stitch to the curve of the patch.

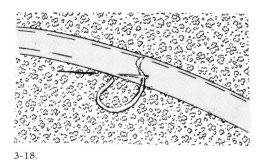

3-18.

Top

The most important step is sewing the quilt blocks together. All corners should be aligned. Sew the blocks, with or without separating strips, into rows and then join each row—again, with or without strips—until the entire quilt top is joined.

Now you are ready to think about your quilting-stitch design. These intricate lines may take many forms. The two quilts shown on page 83 are unusual examples. In the sugar-loaf design the quilting lines continue across the white area in the same diamond pattern as the patch, which was quilted a scant quarter inch from each seam.

The lines must be marked on the quilt top before the quilt is set up if you plan to quilt without a frame. (Quilt frames come with specific instructions.) *The directions given are for quilts made in hoops or in your lap.* Quilt frames make quilting easier, but they take up a lot of space—standing hoops use far less. If your space is at a premium, you can still make a beautiful quilt with an extralarge embroidery hoop or even in your lap.

Follow the instructions for transferring designs given in Chapter 1, marking all borders and strips wider than one inch and filling in plain blocks or large patterns.

To set up the quilt, place the quilt back wrong side up on a flat surface. Place the batting over it and smooth both layers; the batting should be slightly larger than the quilt top. If the batting needs to be pieced, lap the edges one inch and sew the layer together with long, loose running stitches. Finally, place the quilt top right side up over the batting.

Start pinning! Use T-pins or extralong pins. Safety pins may be used if you plan to quilt in your lap without a hoop. Pin through all three layers every four inches or so, working from the center out and smoothing as you go. Your finished work will reflect the care with which the layers were anchored. Baste the layers together—it's the best way to keep them from shifting. Baste diagonally across the quilt from one corner to the other, forming an X; baste around the edges about four inches in; baste every four to six inches across the entire length and width of the quilt (figure 3-19). This basting method is also recommended for machine quilting.

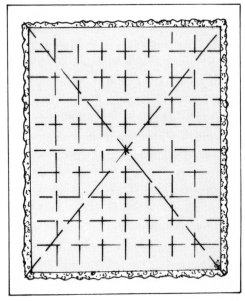

3-19.

Quilting Stitch

A simple running stitch is used. Make about five to nine evenly spaced stitches per inch, depending on the thickness of the quilt. Always work toward yourself. Starting about twelve inches away—a thimble is a must—make a small knot, take a stitch through the top of the quilt only, and pull it through the fabric gently to hide it under the surface. Take two or three stitches, pushing the needle up and down and guiding it with your hand underneath to make sure you are going through all three layers. If there is a thick spot where patches are joined, it may be necessary to take one stitch at a time, inserting the needle through to the back and then reinserting it from the back to the top. Fasten the thread by taking four or five stitches along the ones you have just completed, sewing through the top only. Be sure to test the stitches before starting—make a small sample using the three layers. If you are quilting in a hoop, use an embroidery hoop to practice.

(continued on page 89)

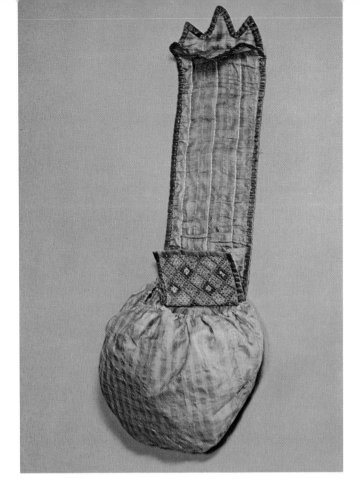

Green silk gingham yarn holder, eighteenth century. *Courtesy of The Brooklyn Museum, The Jason and Peggy Westerfield Collection.*

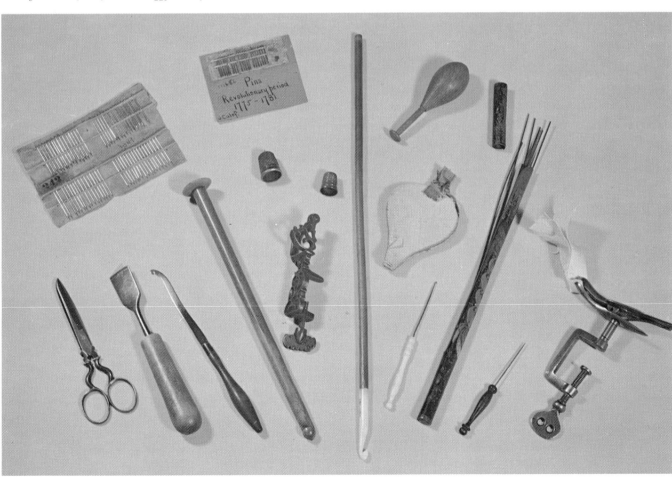

Eighteenth- and nineteenth-century sewing equipment and needlework implements. *Courtesy of Essex Institute, Salem, Mass.*

Linen sampler, made by "IHT," dated 1727. *Courtesy of The Brooklyn Museum, bequest of Margaret S. Bedell.*

Three needlework purses. *Courtesy of Essex Institute, Salem, Mass.*

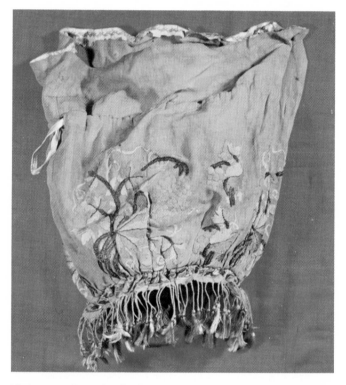

Muslin sewing bag embroidered with silk, early nineteenth century. *Courtesy of Essex Institute, Salem, Mass.*

Bed rug made by Mary Avery of North Andover, signed and dated "M1722A." *Courtesy of Essex Institute, Salem, Mass.*

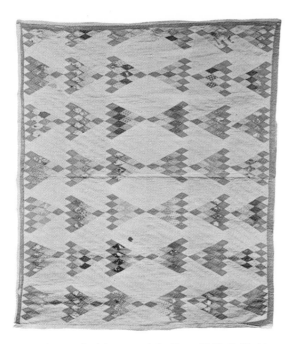

Patchwork quilt, sugar-loaf design, made by Deana DeGodis Washington Hines who was born at Mt. Vernon and lived there for twenty five years. Made in the 1860s. *Courtesy of Smithsonian Institution.*

Indigo blue glazed wool quilted counterpane, made by Esther Wheat who was born in Conway, Mass. Late eighteenth century. *Courtesy of Smithsonian Institution .*

Turkeywork settee, seventeenth century. *Courtesy of Essex Institute, Salem, Mass.*

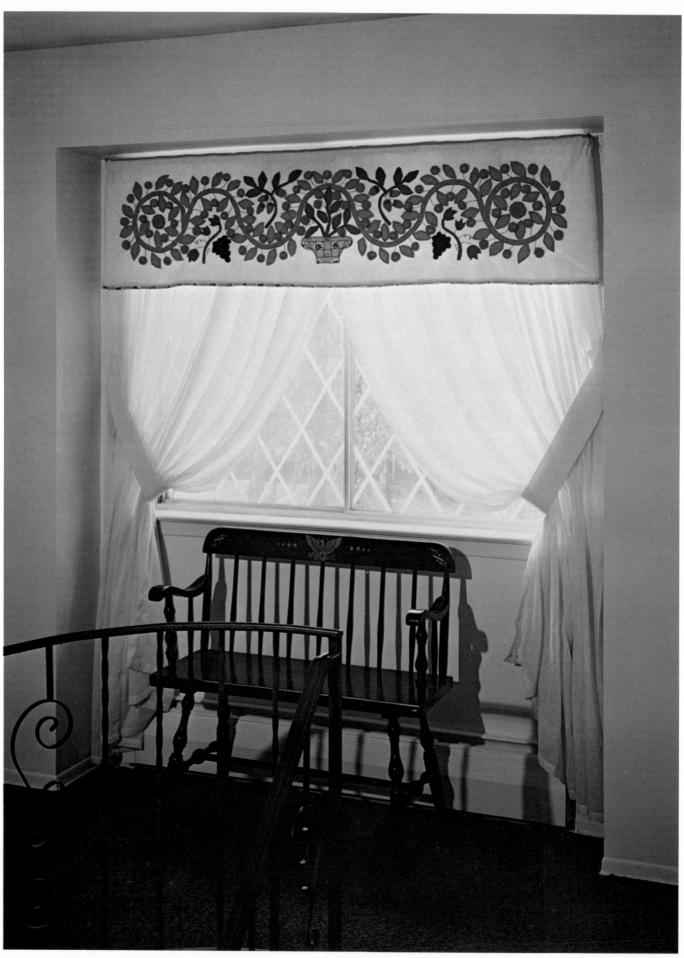

84 Muslin curtains with appliqué valance. *Worked by Adelade Fulger Sullivan and designed by the author.*

Turkeywork handbag. *Designed and worked by the author.*

Patchwork rocking chair back and seat pads. *Designed and worked by the author.*

Braided rug in progress. *Worked by Cathay Z. Fulger.*

Crocheted rug made of socks. *Designed and worked by the author.*

Off-white wool robe with Deerfield Blue embroidery. *Worked by Yvonne Fulger Liebrock and designed by the author.*

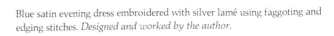
Blue satin evening dress embroidered with silver lamé using faggoting and edging stitches. *Designed and worked by the author.*

White handkerchief-linen blouse with hemstitching and embroidery. Aqua linen skirt with candlewicking. *Designed and worked by the author.*

Stumpwork picture. *Designed and worked by the author.*

"Mandarin Ducks"—Hooked rug made with ⅛" and ¼" wool fabric strips. *Designed and worked by Lib Callaway, New Canaan, Conn.*

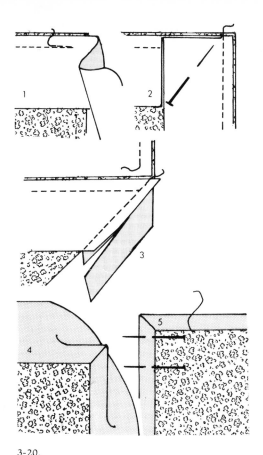

3-20.

Edges

Quilts may be bound with the backing fabric or with bias binding. Since a quarter-inch seam allowance was used throughout, the finished binding should be no more than one-quarter inch wide.

If you are using the backing fabric, trim the batting even with the quilt top. The back should be just long enough to allow for the distance needed to cover the batting and extend one-quarter inch over the quilt top, with one-quarter inch remaining for turning under the raw edge. Trim the back narrower if necessary. Slip-stitch the binding in place, folding in fullness at the corners to miter.

If you are using bias binding, cut one-and-one-quarter-inch strips and piece together as suggested for appliqués (figure 3-16). Trim the batting and the quilt back evenly with the top. Stitch the bias to the quilt with a quarter-inch seam (figure 3-20). End the stitching one-quarter inch from each corner with backstitching (1). Fold the strip diagonally so that the fold is flush with the quilt edge and the bias is running along the other edge. Starting at the edge of the quilt, stitch through the fold and along the entire edge (2). Join the bias with a seam along the straight grain in the same manner as the strip was pieced (3). Turn the binding to the back over the quilt edge, forming a miter at each corner (4). Turn in the raw edge one-quarter inch and form a miter on the back. Slip-stitch the binding in place (5).

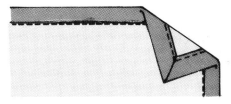

3-21.

The bias may also be stitched in place *by machine*. Follow the five steps shown in figure 3-20 but turn in the raw edge *only* three-sixteenths inch in order to cover the stitches used to sew the binding to the quilt top; form a miter at each corner. From the top, stitch in the groove formed between the bias and the quilt, catching the folded edge underneath (figure 3-21).

(continued from page 80)

Chapter 4

Colonial Rug Making Goes Modern

Rug making was yet another craft invented out of necessity. Enterprising colonists covered the floors of their rough-hewn homes with every available scrap of fabric to protect themselves from splinters and cold winds. Rugs were first used in the East and then were imported to Europe. It must have been the memory of warm carpeting that inspired the original rug designs attributed to these early Americans.

It is unfortunate that so few native rugs remain in existence. They were used until they fell apart—starting in the living room, then relegated to the back door as they faded and used to wipe dirty feet, and probably ending up in the barn to keep a new calf or a litter of puppies warm. Little respect was bestowed upon these handsome works of art that reflected the personality of the homes they adorned. Records of hooked rugs date back to the eighteenth century, as does the beautiful example shown in figure 4-1. Made by Elizabeth Stowell in 1790, this lovely geometric rug could be a focal point in a modern setting, just as it must have been in a colonial room. Unfortunately, braided rugs have not been found dating earlier than the middle 1800s, and crocheted rugs have no historical accounting at all—only word-of-mouth biographies from people like myself. Women in the farming village of Tylersville, Pennsylvania—my mother can trace her family there back to the earliest settlers of Penns Woods— passed these homely rugs down from generation to generation. While I was living in that community as a child, many older women were still making hooked, braided, and crocheted rugs. Our next-door neighbor, Mae Miller, hooked a rug every winter, dyeing her own fabrics with natural materials from her garden. The men in her family drew designs on the reverse side of burlap bags—deer heads, pheasants, and other wildlife; mountain scenes; and domestic animals. Today, it would be hard to find rugs made less than fifty years ago—but I have my neighbor to thank for allowing me to work on her rugs and learn the techniques. I learned a lot about many other crafts she practiced, and her help has stimulated my interest in early American needlecrafts through the years.

4-1. Hooked rug, circa 1790, made by Elizabeth Stowell. *Courtesy of the Metropolitan Museum of Art. Gift of Mrs. Alexander G. Cummins, 1940.*

My mother's busywork also covered a broad spectrum—braided and crocheted rugs, quilting, embroidery, finely crocheted lace, and dressmaking. I got my first "boughten" coat when I was sixteen. The frugal use of all available materials was good training as she raised our family through the depression. We certainly did not feel deprived or under-privileged—she could look into her closet of "goodies" and come up with beautiful gifts and clothes for special occasions.

The fabrics used to make these home-crafted rugs were all recycled, and there is no reason not to continue this practice. Wool produces the most handsome effect, but wool blends and synthetics work equally well. (Knitted fabrics are not suitable for hooked rugs.) You can even use bonded fabrics if you remove the bonding. All recycled and new fabrics should be washed. After washing loosely woven wools, dry them in the dryer at a high temperature to shrink them slightly.

If you don't have any old fabric to recycle, try the thrift shops or ask your friends to save their discards. Watch fabric departments and stores for remnants and sale goods. If you have a special color scheme in mind, it's quite easy to dye these recycled fabrics—just remember that the original color will affect the new color. Sometimes it's a good idea to throw several colors into one harmonizing color bath so they will blend well and be more compatible.

Hooked Rugs

As the months and years passed, colonial men and women sought to improve their homes in many ways. The continuing inaccessibility of supplies, however, forced the settlers to rely on whatever materials were at hand. It is easy to imagine one of these women pondering over narrow strips of fabric that were too small to be sewn together but too pretty to be discarded. What could she do with one-eighth- or one-half-inch strips, six to twelve inches long? Or a woolen garment too thin in spots to be reused as clothing? Some perceptive individual decided to use these scraps to meet the challenge of another hazardous winter and came up with a uniquely contrived, native American floor covering—a hooked rug. The first hooked rugs were probably made with a burlap bag for the foundation—a bag made of flax, hemp, or jute that was used to transport produce. Looped through the foundation with hooks were those narrow fabric strips so carefully saved by prudent craftspeople.

The hooked rug shown in figure 4-2 was probably made in Vermont in the first half of the nineteenth century. The fourteen stars commemorate Vermont's admission into the union. The floral border was done with the colonial techniques described below, and the waves in the background were hooked in rows.

The handsome rug shown on page 88 is a modern example of this colonial technique. Ardent needlecrafters have helped to perpetuate this fascinating but nearly forgotten needle art—just try to purchase a hook in most craft stores and you'll see what I mean.

4-2. American Eagle hooked rug, nineteenth century, probably from Vermont. *Courtesy of the Metropolitan Museum of Art. Rogers Fund, 1945.*

Materials

You will need burlap foundation, fabric that can be cut into strips, heavy-duty or carpet thread, a large-eyed needle, a hook, a padded frame, and T-pins. To estimate how much fabric you will need of each color, place four layers of each color over each design area where it will be used. Medium-weight wool flannel or similar fabric will make a nearly exact duplicate of the colonial originals. Cutting it into strips one-eighth to one-half inch wide was probably busywork for the colonial women—the strips could be stored nearby until they had time to hook the rug. Today, you can purchase a cutting machine that will do the job, saving countless hours. You may lose something, however, with these time-saving methods—the chance to unwind while you meticulously cut each strip. It's not necessary to cut all the strips first—you can cut as you work, and the change of pace is good therapy.

Design

A word of caution for those of you who wish to make your own designs—borders and vertical and horizontal lines must be transferred along a thread of the burlap to ensure that the rug will have straight edges. Curved lines can be executed more easily. Make a design as suggested in Chapter 1 and enlarge it to actual size. Make a stencil by cutting out major sections or by cutting one-eighth-inch-wide slits in the pattern for major motifs or repeats. Use a wide felt-tip pen for transferring the lines. Straight lines for borders can be drawn directly on the burlap, following a thread. The design shown in figure 4-3 is a modified version of the rug shown in figure 4-1—it is easy to transfer to burlap because of its elegant simplicity. A six-inch-wide border surrounds the scallops, which are six inches wide at the base and four inches deep. The colors will make this thirty-by-fifty-one-inch rug outstanding. This design can easily be made larger or smaller to suit your needs. Be sure to allow at least a three-inch margin of burlap around your design for a hem. Turn in the cut edges and sew them in place to prevent fraying.

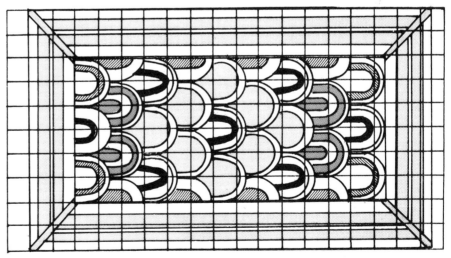

4-3.   each square = 1 inch

Procedure

Use a padded frame and T-pins as explained in Chapter 1 to anchor the burlap as taut as possible. Hold the wooden handle of the hook in the palm of your hand (figure 4-4). Insert the hook into the weave of the burlap and, with your other hand under the burlap, hold the strip up so you can catch it with the hook (1). Pull the strip through, extending the end about one inch above the burlap. Skip a thread and insert the hook again, pulling up a loop one-quarter to three-eighths inch high (2). The looseness of the burlap weave determines how close to place the loops. A heavy bag may need a loop between nearly every thread, while finer burlap (Indian jute) may need a loop every two or three threads. When you come to the end of the fabric strip, pull it to the outside. Start another strip in the same hole. If you have trouble pulling the loop through, press the hook against the threads to make a larger hole and slide the hook along the back of the burlap to hold the strip. As you pull the loop up, the strip should lie flat on the underside (3). Make sure the loop is not twisted on the top. You'll soon find out how easy it is to pull out a loop or to make it longer to eliminate a twist. Practice until the loops are uniform in height and as close together as needed to prevent the burlap from showing. Yarn may be used in place of fabric strips, and the loops may be clipped if desired.

The most effective hooking procedure is to work along the design lines and then fill in the hooked outline. Grass, trees, flowers, and animals look best with a curved shape—it gives them an interesting texture—while borders and geometrics are usually made in rows followng the outlines.

When you have covered the foundation with loops, there is only one more step—hemming the rug. Turn the margin to the wrong side of the rug along the last row of loops, forming a hem. Miter the corners, cutting away excess fabric before sewing the turned-in edges securely together (figure 4-5). Then sew the long edges securely to the rug, using heavy-duty or carpet thread.

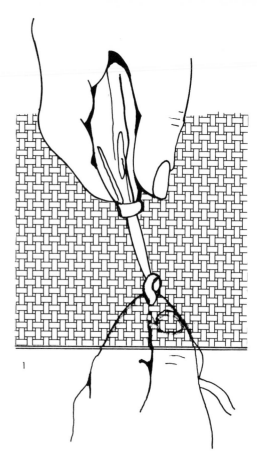

1

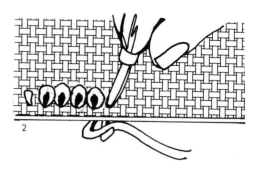

2

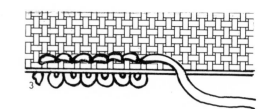

3

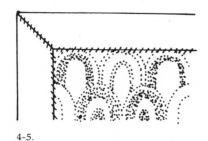

4-5.

Crochet Rugs

The crocheting technique was probably developed in Europe in the sixteenth century as a substitute for lace making with a needle, and it was natural for some of the early settlers to bring a crochet hook as one of the few needlecraft tools that space allowed. Leftover stockings and other soft, pliable fabrics were cut into workable widths and crocheted into simple circles and squares to make homely crochet rugs. Not only are these rugs easy to make—no binding or special finish is required—but mistakes can be quickly pulled out and corrected. The size of the needle and the weight of the "yarn" enable you to complete a rug over a weekend.

Sock "Yarn"

It shouldn't take long to collect enough socks to make a rug. The rug shown in figure 4-6 and in color on page 87 took seventy-one socks. Colorful knitted garments that are faded at the underarm or white T-shirts that you've been saving for cleaning rags will make a great crocheted rug too. Dye the T-shirts to match your decor and work in the other garments for contrast. You may be able to get a good buy on knit remnants at your favorite fabric place—just remember to use the same kind of knit for the entire rug. Cottons and synthetics are usually machine-washable, but wool knits are not.

You are not limited to this design—any instructions for a doily, mat, or afghan can be used to crochet a rug. Simply substitute a size Q crochet hook and sock yarn for the materials specified for the pattern you have selected. The large needle and the heavy yarn will enable you to transform the design into a rug. The same method used to sew braided rugs together (figure 4-16) can be used to sew sock squares together.

4-6.

Sort your socks by color in natural light. Artificial light does strange things to various dark shades, particularly. Separate the socks into bundles by color and cut and join each bundle separately.

To cut a sock into one continuous strip, cut at an angle at the top until the strip is one inch wide (figure 4-7). Cut around the top until you reach the heel—don't worry if the strip is uneven—it will be hidden when it is crocheted. Cut along the top of the worn heel spot and then to the right of it, allowing a one-inch strip beyond the hole. Continue cutting the foot into strips until you reach the toe. Cut away any worn spot the same way as for the heel. Now go back and cut the worn heel section to the same width.

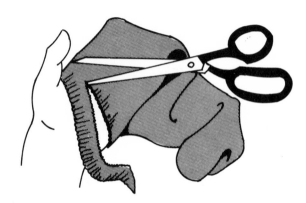

4-7.

If some of your socks are thinner or heavier than the rest, cut the thin ones into slightly wider strips and the heavy ones into narrower strips.

To join sock strips (figure 4-8), make a one-quarter-inch slash about one inch from both ends of each strip (1). Pull one strip end through the slash in another strip. To fasten them together, pull the opposite end of the inserted strip through its own slash (2). Pull both strips gently until the ends lie flat (3). Fasten the ribbed top of one strip to the toe of another so the texture of the "yarn" is consistent throughout the rug. Roll the strips into balls for easy storage, stretching them so they curl as you wind. If you are using knitted fabric, cut the strips crosswise (or around the body shape)—the raw edges will curl in better, and the strips will be more flexible.

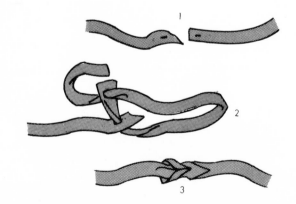

4-8.

4-9.

Procedure

Develop a rhythm as you crochet with the large needle and the thick sock yarn. Insert the needle all the way through the stitch until the fattest portion of the needle has penetrated, then pull the loop through, making it as large as the fat shank of the hook. Always complete the stitch with a loop as large as the hook shank. It may be easier to throw the yarn into the hook when you need more yarn.

To start the rug (figure 4-9), make a slip knot on the hook, forming a loop (1). Hold the knot between the thumb and middle finger of your left hand (if you are right-handed). Wrap the yarn around your little finger and extend it over your index finger. Pass the hook under, then over the yarn (2). Draw the yarn through the loop, forming another loop (3). Make a chain with three more loops to make a four-loop chain (4). Slip-stitch the ends together by inserting the hook into the first loop by the knot and pull the yarn through both loops (5), forming a ring. Make two chains (6).

Row 1: Make a single crochet over the ring by passing the hook into the ring (7). Pull the yarn through the ring, making a second loop on the hook (8). Pass the hook under, then over the yarn, pulling it through both loops (9), to complete the single crochet. Make four or more single crochets loosely over the ring (two chains count as one single crochet, so you will have a total of six stitches.) Slip-stitch the last single crochet on the top stitch of the two chains (10).

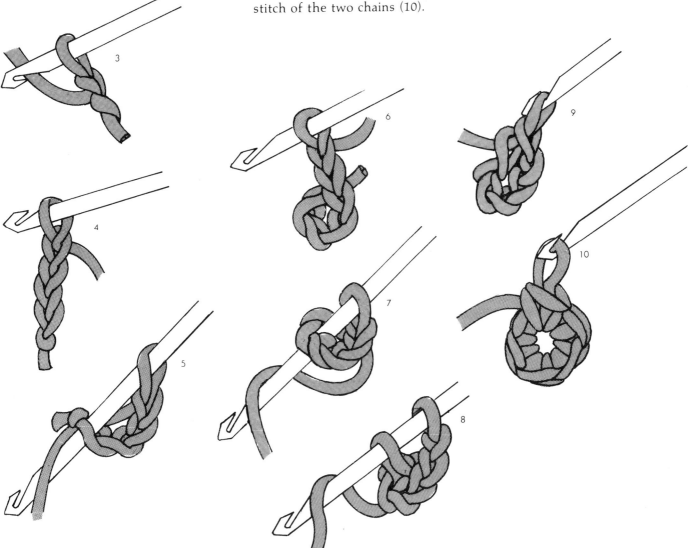

Row 2: Make two chains, a single crochet in the first stitch of the chain, and two single crochets in each of the next five stitches loosely around the ring (a total of twelve stitches, counting two chains as one single crochet). Slip-stitch the row together. The work may "cup" slightly, but the next row will flatten it out.

Row 3: This row starts the hexagonal shaping. Make two chains to form the corner. *Make one single crochet, two chains, one single crochet* in the next single crochet (passing the hook under the two upper strands) of row 2. Make a single crochet in the next stitch. Repeat the instructions between the asterisks five more times, with a single crochet between each corner. You should have six corners and six single crochets (two chains count as one single crochet). Slip-stitch the last corner to two chains, forming a hexagon.

Row 4: Make two chains, a single crochet in the first single crochet in row 3, and a corner over the two-chain space. *Make one single crochet, two chains, one single crochet,* then make one single crochet in the next three stitches of row 3. Repeat the pattern between the asterisks four times. Make a corner over the two-chain space with a single crochet, two chains, and a single crochet; make a single crochet in the last stitch of row 3. You should have six corners with three single crochets between each. Slip-stitch the row together. End by cutting the yarn end to three inches and pull the end through the loop tightly to fasten.

Row 5: Using another color, start the yarn at the opposite side of the hexagon. Pull a loop through a single crochet at the center, leaving a three- or four-inch end on the wrong side of the rug. Holding the end along the back of the single-crochet upper strands, make two chains. Make one single crochet in the next two stitches of row 4, then make the corner—*one single crochet, two chains, one single crochet*—over the two-chain space, working over the strip too. Make one single crochet in the next four stitches of row four and make the corner four more times. Make a corner, then make one single crochet in the last stitch of row four. You should have six corners with four single crochets between each. Slip-stitch the row together. Make two chains.

Continue making the rug in this manner, always adding one single crochet on each side of the hexagon for every row. Make the rug as large as desired. Your objectives should be a flat rug. Since you are working with an unknown, it is difficult to give hard and fast instructions. If the rug starts to cup, add another single crochet on each side of the hexagon. If it ripples, decrease a single crochet on each side by skipping a single crochet on the previous row.

Place the rug wrong side up and stretch at the opposite edges to pull it into shape. The socks are quite flexible, and the rug can easily be coaxed into shape.

Braided Rugs

The need to cover floors as protection from the elements is no longer a reason for the continued interest in this fascinating home craft, although braided rugs retain the qualities deemed so necessary by early American women. A lofty rug, with many thicknesses twisted and sewn together in a uniform fashion, complements contemporary furniture and gives pleasure to the barefooted. Braided rugs are enjoying a revival.

These rugs can be as thrifty or as elegant as you desire. Old rags and garments, cotton, wool, or blends may be used, or you may find some bargain fabric that will make a most handsome rug. A polyester knit would make an outstanding rug. Just remember to wash all fabric before using it to remove soil or sizing. Figure 4-10 shows a braided rug in progress. It is also shown in color on page 87.

4-10.

Preparation

Make a test braid to determine how wide to cut or tear the fabric strips: one-and-one-quarter- to two-inch-wide strips usually work best; depending on the fabric weight. Be sure to use the same weight throughout, or you may have thick and thin spots, and do not use stiff or slippery fabrics. Soft, medium- to heavyweight, firmly woven fabrics, such as wool flannel or polyester knits, will make sturdy, durable rugs.

The only other supplies you need are approximately forty inches of heavy yarn, some heavy carpet thread, large-eyed crewel darning needles, a thimble, and a large safety pin. To estimate the fabric requirements, plan on three-fourths to one pound per square foot. Fabric may be redyed to suit.

Cut the strips and sew them together as you braid (figure 4-11). Anything longer than fifty-four to sixty inches tangles and will slow you down. Crosswise (selvage to selvage) strips work best, as they have more give. Cut the ends diagonally to distribute the bulk at the seams (1), join the ends (2), and finger-press the seam open (3).

The instructions below explain how to fold as you braid. Some rugcrafters, however, like to press the fabric into soft folds. Individual strips can be rolled in a ball or stored in bags by color. Don't try to cut all the strips at one time.

Braiding

Select three colors or three matching strips, each a different length—seams must be staggered to make the braids a consistent width throughout (figure 4-12). The diagram shows a gray, a white, and a plaid braid so you can follow the procedure easily—follow the same order with the three strips you have selected. Seam two colors or strips together. Turn in the raw edges to meet at the center of the third strip and the seamed strips, and baste (1). Stitch heavy yarn through all the layers and knot. Slip the yarn over your foot to hold the braid firmly. Start braiding by folding the gray strip over the black strip (2). Fold the plaid strip over the gray strip (3). Bring the black strip up and over the plaid strip (4). Continue alternating strips in this manner, adding to the strips as necessary. Secure all three strips together with a safety pin to prevent unraveling when you lay your work aside (5).

4-12.

To fold each strip as you braid, press the center of the strip down with your thumb, turning the edges in toward the thumb with your first and second fingers. With both edges turned in, fold the strip down the center. The tighter the tension on the braid, the easier it is to fold and braid. Keep double-folded edges to the right and single folds to the left for smooth braids. Knit fabrics fold easier if they are used wrong side out. Shorten the yarn as the work progresses. When the braid is long enough, hold it down with your foot and remove the yarn. Roll the braids up in balls to store.

There are many ways to construct the braids. You can make them in one continuous strip, with defined borders or bands, a combination of the two methods—spiraling the center and joining the border—or a row at a time. Just have a plan in mind—and you can start whenever you have collected enough strips of one color or equal amounts of three colors.

To finish the ends of a continuous braid, simply taper the ends of each strip for about twelve inches. When the braid is sewn together in a rug, the outer edge will blend in smoothly.

To make a simple joining, wrap a thread securely around each end of the braid, allowing a little overlap. Cut the strips to about three inches (figure 4-13). Work the strips back into the braid with a crochet hook and trim (1). Remove the thread and sew the ends together invisibly (2).

4-13.

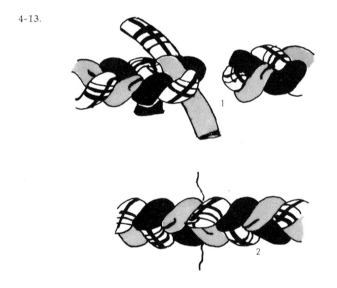

Continuous bands of braids can be manipulated to form a perfect joining (figure 4-14). Keep each strip flat and avoid twisting. Join one of the colors in a diagonal seam (1). Join the second color in a diagonal seam (2). Join the last color, shifting the individual strips up or down the braid to eliminate any slack (3). To join a solid braid, mark each strip and proceed in the same manner.

When you have finished your braids and joined them together, it is time to sew them into a rug. To start a round rug, roll the braid into a tight coil. For an oval rug make a short loop, and for an oblong rug start with a straight strip.

4-14.

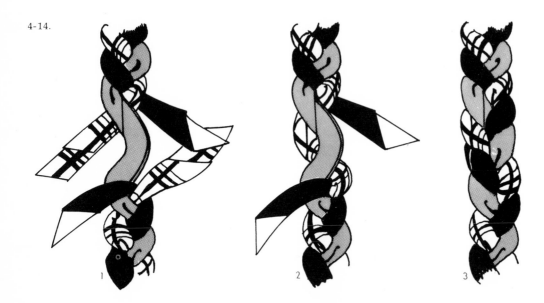

Work on a table from right to left. Form the center of the rug by spiraling the braids tightly, keeping them flat (figure 4-15). When the braids are shaped perfectly, hold the starting coils firmly between your fingers. Pinch the braids together so the two edges are uppermost and overcast the edges together securely with carpet thread (figure 4-16). Work a short distance, then lay the rug back down on the table, pressing the sewn area gently with the palms of your hands to make the braids lie flat and to hide the stitches. Some shapes may require easing: work in fullness smoothly. Repeat this procedure—coil, pinch, sew, press—until the entire rug is sewn together.

4-15.

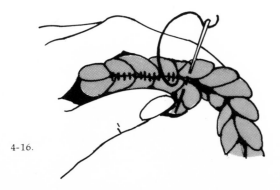

4-16.

4-17.

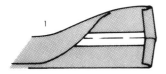

4-18.

Extralarge rugs must be made on the floor. Sit on a low stool and place a heavy piece of cardboard over your outstretched legs for a flat working surface. Move around the rug as you work.

Store the rug on a flat surface when you are not working—folding it may distort the shape.

You can make lovely place mats or rectangular rugs by joining equal lengths of braid in the same manner (figure 4-17). Sew across the braid two or three inches beyond the ends by hand or machine. To finish the strands (figure 4-18), turn in the ends of each strand (1) and sew together (2).

These basic techniques were selected to get you started. By the time your first braided rug is completed, I'm sure you will think of many more unique adaptations of this fantastic early American home craft.

Chapter 5

Projects

Any of the basic designs provided in this chapter can be embellished with nearly all of the needle arts explained in Chapters 2, 3, and 4. Crewelwork, openwork, whitework, candlewicking, stumpwork, bargello, turkeywork, appliqué, patchwork, and rug hooking will all work well.

Pocketbook

The construction of this pocketbook was adapted from the lovely flamestitched bargello pocketbook shown on page 82.

Materials

You will need a completed rectangle of needlework seven and one-half inches by ten and one-half inches with a half-inch seam allowance on all edges. (If you are using embroidery, allow enough fabric to hold the rectangle securely in the hoop. Canvas should have at least a one-inch margin all around. Burlap must be large enough to pin to a padded frame. Patchwork and appliqué rectangles should have a half-inch seam allowance on all outer edges.) You will also need one and one-quarter yards of half-inch-wide fold-over braid; one-quarter yard of durable lining fabric, such as the quality used for coats and jackets; one rectangle of stiffening eight and one-half inches by eleven and one-half inches (crinoline or heavy interfacing). Openwork rectangles will need a backing so the stiffening won't show through; use a lightweight fabric in a matching or contrasting color.

Pattern

On your fabric or canvas draw a rectangle seven and one-half inches by ten and one-half inches, rounding the corners at one end. Draw one line three inches from the rounded end; draw another one-half inch further away. (This small strip is the slack needed to cover the pocket.) This rectangle section is the pattern for the top flap that closes the pocketbook. Now draw a line three and one-half inches from the straight end—this will be the front, and the remaining section will be the back.

Create a design with these three divisions in mind and transfer it to the foundation fabric or canvas. Remember that the worked surface is quite small—choose a simple design. Figure 5-1 shows a flame-stitch pattern adapted from the original, which was worked on a very fine mono canvas. The design is repeated throughout. Use a connecting row of black or a dark-colored tapestry yarn for each outline. Be sure to place the highest stitch of the diamond outline at the center of your canvas, along the line marking the outline for the bargello. Notice the variegated shades and select your yarn accordingly, using two or more shaded colors with a row of off-white at the base of the pattern and two shades of another color for the diamond motif.

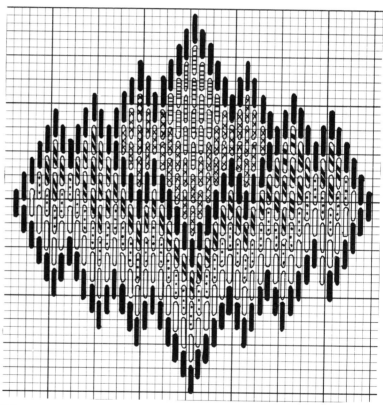

5-1.

Lining

When the needlework design is completed, trim the excess foundation fabric or canvas to within one-half inch of the marked rectangle. Cut an eight-and-one-half-inch-by-eleven-and-one-half-inch rectangle of stiffening (the seventeeth-century pocketbook was stiffened with cardboard), shaping one end to match the foundation. Cut two lining sections and a backing section for openwork the same size as the stiffening.

In one lining section (figure 5-2) cut an opening five inches long and one-half inch wide about two inches from the cut edge of the shaped end, rounding the corners of the opening (1). Cut a straight strip of lining fabric one inch wide and fourteen inches long. Fold this strip in half lengthwise and press lightly (2). Turn in both raw edges to meet the fold and press again (3). Open out the binding folds and turn in one end one-half inch as you pin the binding to the opening, with the raw edges even and the right sides together. Extend the remaining end over the turned-in end and trim to one-quarter inch. Sew in place along the crease, pulling the rounded lining corners nearly straight as you stitch (4). At the corners clip the lining *only* to the stitches. Turn the binding to the inside over the seam and pin, stretching the corners so the folded edge of the binding will lie flat—don't expect it to be absolutely flat. Slip-stitch the remaining folded edge of the binding in place (5).

5-2.

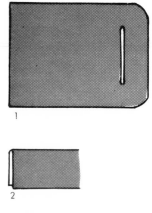

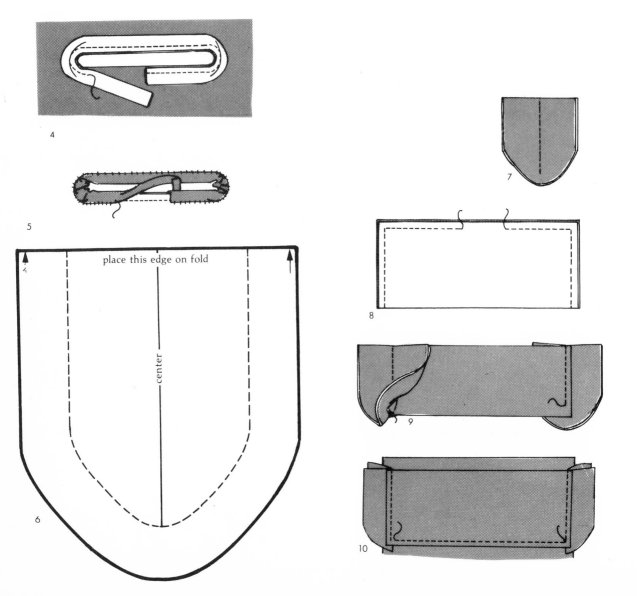

place this edge on fold

center

To make end gussets and a divider, trace the gusset pattern (6). Cut two gussets from fabric folded wrong sides together. Baste the cut edges together in a half-inch seam. Fold the gusset in half along the center line and press to form a crease, which will be used as a stitching guide (7). Cut a rectangle seven and one-half inches wide and nine inches long. Fold it in half, wrong sides together, and stitch in a half-inch seam, leaving an opening for turning it right side out. (8). Turn the right side out through the opening and press. Slip-stitch the opening shut. Place the gussets under the divider, with each narrow end extending one-quarter inch over the center crease and the lower edge extending one-quarter inch beyond the gusset seamline. Sew the ends securely in place along the center, ending at the seamline (9). Turn the straight end of the lining section, with the opening up, three and one-half inches; press the fold to form a crease for a stitching guide. Place the divider over the crease, with the lower edge extending one-quarter inch beneath it. (The top edge of the divider should be one-half inch below the straight edge of the lining.) Sew securely in place along the guideline, keeping the gussets free (10).

Assembly

Place the needlework section wrong side up; place the stiffening over the needlework, matching the shaped corners. If you are using backing, place it wrong side up between the needlework and the stiffening. Position the plain lining section over the stiffening, right side up, matching the shaped corners (figure 5-3). Place the remaining lining section over the other layers (the opening forms a large pocket), match the shaped corners, and baste through all thicknesses, keeping the gussets free (1). Form the pocketbook by basting the gussets in place, with the folded edge of the gusset one-half inch below the straight end. Encase all edges with half-inch-wide fold-over braid; miter the corners; ease the braid to fit the shaped corners, turning in the ends where they meet on the straight end; and baste. Sew the braid securely in place. Fasten the flap with three snaps (2). Simple snap fasteners were not usually available to the colonists, so they used a tie closure—any fastener can be used, even an elastic loop and a button.

5-3.

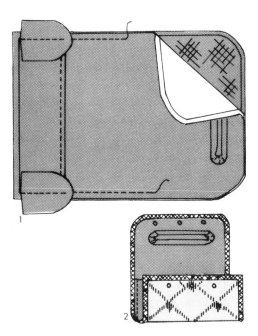

Change Purse

This simple envelope-style purse is a miniversion of the bargello pocketbook and could be made to match and carried inside. The needlecraft used to decorate the foundation should be fairly flat if you wish to slip it into a small, flat handbag. The unpretentious white silk purse shown on page 82 was richly embroidered with gold thread couching and tiny flowers.

Materials

You will need a completed rectangle of needlework three and one-half inches by seven inches with a quarter-inch seam allowance on all edges. (If you are using embroidery, allow enough fabric to hold the rectangle securely in the hoop. Canvas should have at least a one-inch margin all around. Patchwork and appliqué rectangles should have a quarter-inch seam allowance on all outer edges.) As with the larger purse you will also need a four-by-seven-and-one-half-inch rectangle of durable lining fabric, such as the quality used for coats and jackets, and a rectangle of stiffening four inches by seven and one-half inches (crinoline or heavy interfacing). Openwork rectangles will need a backing so the stiffening won't show through: use a lightweight fabric in a matching or contrasting fabric.

Pattern

Draw a rectangle three and one-half inches by seven inches and round the corners at one end. Draw a line one and three-quarters inches from the rounded end—this is the top flap that closes the purse—then draw a line two and one-half inches from the straight end for the purse front. The middle section is the back and should be the most decorative. Decide on a design and transfer it to the foundation fabric—do *not* transfer the dividing lines. When the needlework is completed, trim the excess foundation fabric to one-quarter inch of the marked outline. Canvas should *not* be trimmed—follow the instructions below for a canvas purse.

Fabric Purse

Cut a four-inch-by-seven-and-one-half-inch rectangle of stiffening and a rectangle of lining fabric (and of backing fabric for openwork) the same size, shaping one end to match the foundation. Baste the stiffening to the wrong side of the needlework. If you are using backing, place it wrong side up between the needlework and the stiffening. Pin the lining and the needlework right sides together. Stitch through all thicknesses in a quarter-inch seam, beginning and ending one-half inch from each end of the straight end to leave an opening for turning (figure 5-4). Trim and grade the seams to reduce bulk in the seam allowance (1). Turn the fabric right side out through the opening, press, and slip-stitch the opening at the straight end (2). Fold up the straight end two and one-half inches to form the pocket and sew the ends securely in place with slip-stitches (3). Fasten the flap with a snap or with a button and buttonhole. Work an edgestitch (Chapter 2) along the ends and the flap if desired.

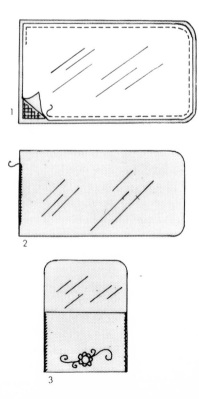

5-4.

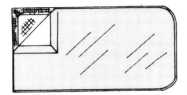

Canvas Purse

Turn in the edges along the embroidery and press firmly with your fingers. Trim the excess canvas at the corners and sew the corners to the canvas (figure 5-5). Cut a rectangle of lining fabric one-quarter inch larger than the embroidery on all edges. Turn in the lining edges one-quarter inch and slip-stitch (figure 3-8) to the canvas. Form the pocket and sew the ends in place as with the fabric purse.

Shoulder Bag

Figure 5-6 shows another lovely pocketbook you can make, this one embroidered with turkeywork.

Materials

You will need a fourteen-by thirty-inch rectangle of penelope rug canvas, seven meshes to the inch, and a strip of the same canvas four by fourteen inches for the strap; seven-eighths yard of lining fabric; a seven-inch zipper; three-ply Persian tapestry yarn—about five ounces luggage tan, four ounces each light navy blue and bright orange, three ounces moss green, two ounces each natural (off-white), dark brown, and beige; and seven or more assorted (sizes 18 to 21) blunt-point tapestry needles.

5-6.

Pattern

To prevent the canvas from fraying, encase the cut edges with tape. Draw a line along a set of double threads at the center of the canvas. All stitches are done on the pair of threads separating the meshes.

Using the graphs shown in figures 5-7 and 5-8 as a guide, mark off sixty-seven sets of double threads (the bag is about ten inches wide) for the front edge of the bag, about one inch from the narrow end of the canvas. Following the graph, mark off the front about six and seven-eighths inches; bottom, three inches; back, six and seven-eighths inches; and flap, eight and one-half inches, tapering to four and five-eighths inches so it will fit under the strap. You can use waterproof felt-tip pens in corresponding colors to transfer the design from the graph to the canvas. Mark the color on the inner edges of each set of double threads.

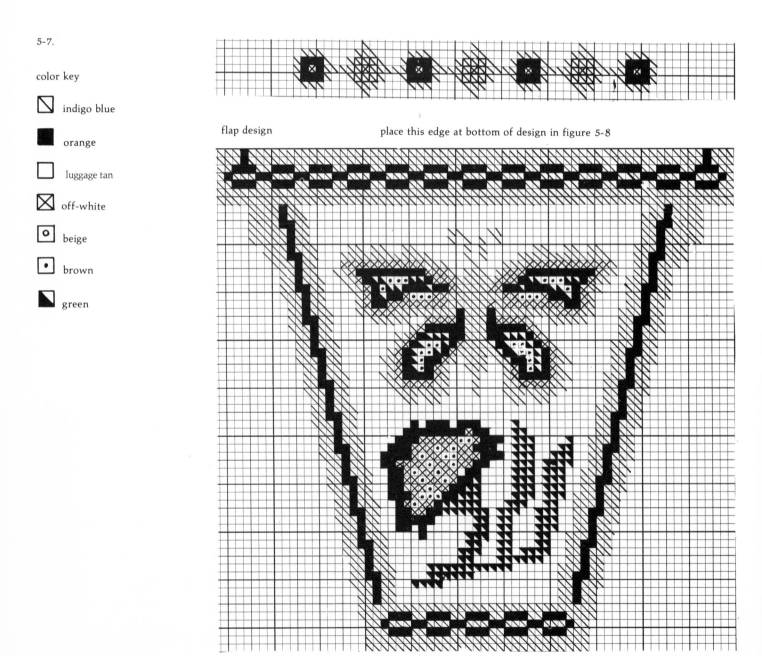

5-7.

color key

◩ indigo blue

◼ orange

☐ luggage tan

⊠ off-white

⊡ beige

⊡ brown

◢ green

flap design   place this edge at bottom of design in figure 5-8

110

center strap over rectangle

Design

You can use any color combination you wish for the turkeywork embroidery—the colors shown were the most popular and the easiest to acquire in colonial days. Indigo blue (light navy) was a favorite for some time and was used quite extensively, as was "mad redder brown" (luggage tan), so they were used as the main colors for the handbag. By the time you complete the first row you'll have mastered the turkeywork stitch (figure 2-68). For speedier coverage thread a needle for each color. I used as many as eighteen needles at one time, working with as many needles as I needed for each color of yarn for each row—some colors had three to six threaded needles each. In this fashion I could do all the clipping at one time. Use the yarn to the last inch, inserting the needle eye first to complete the stitch when ending the yarn.

Work the bag front until you reach the rectangle marked for the strap. Do not work the threads at each end of the rectangle—work the marked area with turkeywork stitch, pulling the loops flat like the knot. This will cover the canvas with matching yarn and allow space to tuck in the flap for a closure.

When this area is embroidered, make the strap. Transfer the design to the center of the four-by-fourteen-inch canvas strip. Fold the long canvas edges under along a set of double threads, leaving a nine-mesh-wide strap (one mesh on each side of the pattern will be used to whipstitch the edges). Use a mesh to form the fold and line up the meshes in all three layers. Work the pattern for the length indicated through all three layers, inserting the needle through the layers and bringing it back to the outside.

Whipstitch the edges (figure 2-69). You will need two sets of double threads. Place the strap over the embroidered rectangle and baste the canvas ends to the canvas foundation, matching meshes. Continue working the pattern through all four canvas layers.

Lining

Make a pattern for the lining by tracing the exact measurement of the embroidered area, using the wrong side of the canvas as a guide (figure 5-9). Add a one-inch seam allowance on all edges. For the pockets cut two six-by-nine-inch rectangles and one nine-by-twelve-inch rectangle. Stitch the two smaller rectangles together with a half-inch seam, leaving an opening for turning on one edge (1). Turn the fabric right side out through the opening and press. Slip-stitch the opening shut. Reinforce one long edge with two rows of machine stitching, one row one-eighth inch from the top edge, the other one-quarter inch away (2). Cut two two-inch squares of lining fabric. Fold them in half, wrong sides together, and press. Baste one to each end of the zipper, with folded edges in (3). Turn in the short ends of the remaining section one-half inch and press. Place the folded-pocket edges of the lining over the zipper tape about one-eighth inch from the teeth and stitch together (4). Open the zipper and turn the lining wrong side out. Fold it along the edge of the zipper tape and stitch the ends (5). Turn it right side out through the zipper and press. Make two rows of stitching to reinforce, again one-eighth inch and one-quarter inch from the top of the pocket (6). Position the pockets on the lining one inch below the top of the front and back. Machine-stitch in place one-eighth inch and one-quarter inch from the side and lower edges (7).

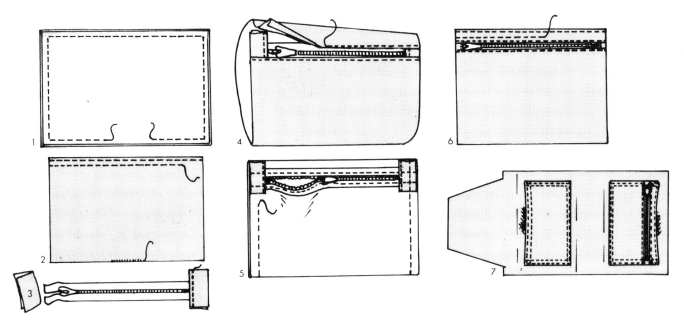

To attach the lining, pin it to the canvas over the turkeywork, right sides together (figure 5-10). With the canvas uppermost stitch along the third mesh from the embroidery (you need two sets of double threads to whipstitch the edges after the lining is attached), starting at the center of the narrow flap end and ending one inch beyond the corner on the front edge (1). Remove the pins and extend the lining one-half inch beyond its original position so it will not bubble when turned right side out—the canvas may "bow" slightly. Stitch the remaining long edge and ends in the same manner. Trim the canvas to one-half inch, removing the tape and clipping the inner corners to the stitching (2). Turn it right side out and press lightly. Whipstitch all exposed canvas edges as before, again using two sets of double threads. Then slip-stitch the remaining front lining edge in place (3).

5-10.

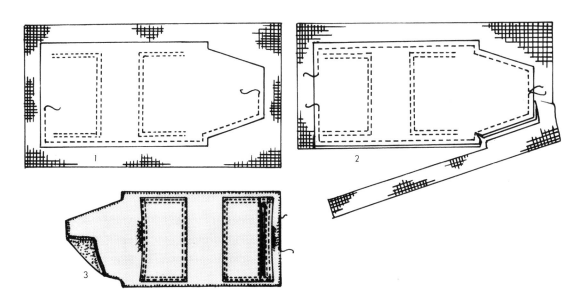

Handle

To make the handle, you will need machine needles for leather, cotton-wrapped polyester-core thread, thirty inches of half-inch cable cord, and a strip of leather six inches by forty-one inches (pieced together if necessary).

On the wrong side of the leather mark one strip three inches wide and forty-one inches long for the handle, two strips three inches wide and twelve inches long for the ends, and two strips three inches wide and eight inches long for the rings. Cut out the pieces with very sharp scissors.

To form the rings (figure 5-11), lap the ends one-half inch and stitch (1). Fold each ring in half and crease flat, using scissor handles (2). Turn in the free edges to meet the fold. Flatten the two folds and stitch together, close to the double-folded edges (3). To form the ends, insert the narrow end through the ring and fold down so the end measures eight and one-half inches. Stitch one-quarter inch from the cut edge, and again one and one-half inches from the edge folded over the ring (4).

5-11.

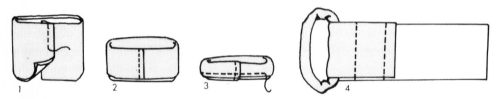

To form the handle, cut the ends on a slant so the seam won't be too bulky. (Make seams for piecing the same way.) Slip the ends through the rings, making sure that the right sides of the ends are facing up (figure 5-12). Lap the ends one-half inch and stitch (1). Fold the handle flat. With the edges even, stitch down the center of the strip, starting and ending two inches from the fold over the ring. Backstitch to reinforce (2). To stabilize the handle, insert the cable cord in each side and turn the raw edges one-quarter inch to one-half inch opposite the center stitching, allowing the raw edges to taper out near the ring. Stitch close to the folded edges, encasing the cord (3).

5-12.

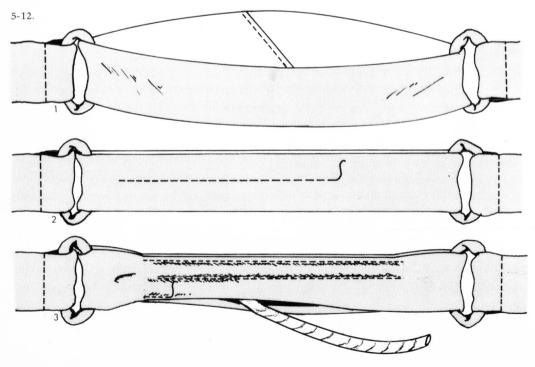

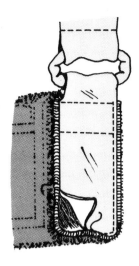

5-13.

Sew the ends to the bag by placing the top row of stitching even with the whipped edge. From the leather side, stitch down the long edge and around the corner to the center of the narrow end (figure 5-13). Break the stitches and do the same for the other long edge. The bag will be cumbersome under the machine when you stitch the second side, but crush gently—it's quite pliable. Complete the bag by stitching the remaining end in place.

Drawstring Bag

This purse is a modified version of the lovely blue velvet evening bag shown on page 82. The original had a silk top that has started to disintegrate; the velvet was appliquéd with crewel embroidery. The lovely muslin sewing bag shown on page 82 had a two-inch self-fringe with one-inch silk tassels. The bag itself was made from a rectangle about eighteen inches wide and thirty inches long, with a round nine-inch bottom. The lightly quilted bottom had a paper batting. The edges were turned up, and the bag gathered to fit. Lined with pale green silk that was feather-stitched to the top of the bag, it had gathered pockets along the bottom edges to hold smaller items, and a flannel rectangle was sewn in the seam to hold needles. If you want to make a bag using your favorite stitches, follow the instructions for the drawstring bag, enlarging the measurements accordingly.

Pattern

Draw a rectangle eight inches by fourteen inches, and within the rectangle draw in a half-inch seam allowance along the two sides and the bottom long edge. On the remaining top edge draw a line one and one-half inches below for a fold. Add two more lines one-half inch and three-quarters inch apart for stitching lines. In the exact center of the lines draw a vertical line for a buttonhole. Create a design for your bag between the seamlines and the lower stitching, an area five and three-quarters inches by twelve inches. Transfer the pattern to the fabric—do *not* transfer the seamlines. Allow enough extra fabric to hold the rectangle in a hoop if you are using embroidery. For patchwork make a rectangle the same size, planning seam allowances or borders as desired.

Assembly

To make a buttonhole in the casing, baste a one-and-one-half-inch square of firm or matching fabric under the line (figure 5-14). Make a slit the length of the line and work buttonhole stitch (figure 2-16) around the slit, fanning the ends (1). Join the short rectangle ends to form a tube—stitch in a half-inch seam, leaving an opening for the drawstring between the two stitching lines. Press the seam open (2). Turn the top edge to the inside along the fold line and pin. To form the casing, stitch along both stitching lines from the outside. Make a row of gathering stitches one-half inch from the remaining edge (3). Cut a circle of the foundation fabric three and one-half inches in diameter—why not embroider the date on the circle, as that enterprising woman did in 1764, and then add your name or initials before cutting it out? Mark this circle and the bag in quarters with pins. With the right sides together, pin the bag to the circle, matching the pins. Pull up the gathering thread gently to fit, tie the thread ends, and distribute fullness evenly. Sew the bag to the foundation circle along the gathering thread in a half-inch seam (4).

5-14.

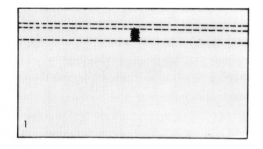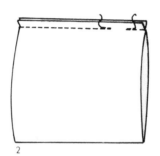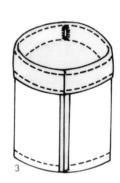

Lining

Cut a five-and-three-quarters-inch-by-thirteen-inch rectangle and a circle three and one-half inches in diameter of lining fabric. Stitch the ends of the rectangle in a seam and press open. Gather and stitch this tube to the circle in the same manner as for the bag. Turn in the remaining edge one-half inch and baste. Turn the bag wrong side out and slip the lining right side out over it. Slip-stitch (figure 3-18) the folded lining edge to the bag along the lower stitching line. Turn the bag right side out.

Drawstrings

Use two eighteen-inch lengths of one-quarter-inch decorative cord or make drawstrings with self- or lining fabric. To make the drawstrings, cut two one-and-one-quarter-inch-wide strips eighteen inches long. Fold each strip in half lengthwise and press. Turn in the cut edges to meet the fold and press again. Sew the folded edges together. Insert one drawstring into the casing through an opening in the seam, using a safety pin; knot the ends together. Insert the remaining drawstring into the casing through the buttonholes and knot the ends. Pull the drawstrings to close (figure 5-15).

5-15.

116

Basic Skirt

This easy-to-make skirt consists of two fabric panels, and it can be any length or width you desire. To estimate yardage, each panel should be the desired length plus a three-inch hem allowance and a two- to six-inch "shrinkage" allowance for the needlework. The aqua skirt shown on page 85 lost two inches in length due to the candlewicking embroidery. A quilted skirt such as the one shown in figure 5-24 may shrink four to six inches regardless of which quilting method is used. Double the amount needed for one panel and add three and one-quarter inches for a waistband (one inch wide when finished). If you are using thirty-six-inch-wide fabric, add another four inches to the length for the placket. Colonial women made a six-inch slash for a skirt placket and encased the edge in a fine twill tape, sewn securely by hand.

Design

Transfer your chosen design to each panel as explained in Chapter 1, making sure that the lines will match when the five-eighths-inch seam is stitched. Decide whether you want the needlework to end at the hem edge or several inches above it.

Assembly

Join the panels with a five-eighths-inch seam. Complete your needlework design. Turn up the hem evenly at the lower edge and pin. Hold the skirt up to you to see if it is too long or too short. Adjust the hem width or cut away any excess length at the top. Clean-finish the raw hem edge with seam binding or zigzag the edge. Sew the hem in place.

Placket

Cut a four-by-eleven-inch strip of fabric (figure 5-16). Draw a line six and five-eighths inches long at the center of the strip, starting at one end. Clean-finish the long edges and the unmarked end by turning them in one-quarter inch and stitching or zigzagging the raw edges. Center the placket over the center of one panel, with the right sides together and the upper edges even, and pin. Stitch around the line, one-eighth inch from each side, tapering to a point at the end (1). Cut along the line to the end of the stitching. Turn the placket inside and press. To reinforce, stitch along the opening edges, one-eighth inch beyond them (2).

5-16.

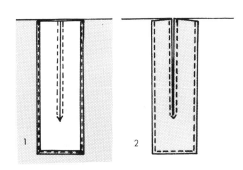

Pleat Waist

Form a two-inch pleat over the placket opening and pin (figure 5-17). Pleat the upper edge to fit your waist measurement plus one-half inch to allow for the bulk of the seam allowances and pleats. Baste the pleats in place with pins or thread. The pleat over the placket may be adjusted to correspond to the width of the other pleats. The skirt may be gathered if desired.

5-17.

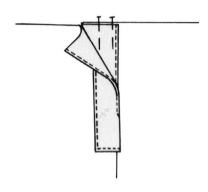

Waistband

Cut a strip three and one-quarter inches wide and the length of your waist plus three-quarters inch for wearing ease, the length of the underneath layer of the pleat (two inches unless it was adjusted), and one and one-quarter inches for seam allowances, a total of four additional inches. Fold the waistband in half lengthwise and stitch the ends in a five-eighths-inch seam. Trim the ends, turn, and press. Pin the right side of the waistband to the wrong side of the skirt, placing one end even with the folded edge of the pleat over the placket and the remaining end even with the placket edge next to the body (figure 5-18). Stitch in place. Pull the waistband up and press the seam. Turn in the remaining long edge five-eighths inch and pin in place, enclosing the seam. Stitch the folded edge in place through all thicknesses (1). Fasten the waistband with hooks and eyes, and the placket with snaps (2).

5-18.

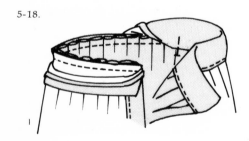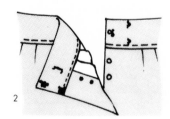

Candlewick Skirt

To make a candlewick skirt (figure 5-19), follow the basic skirt instructions above, allowing two or three inches more than the desired length to compensate for needlework "shrinkage." Be sure to shrink the fabric when the embroidery is completed but before the waistband is attached to hold the tufts securely.

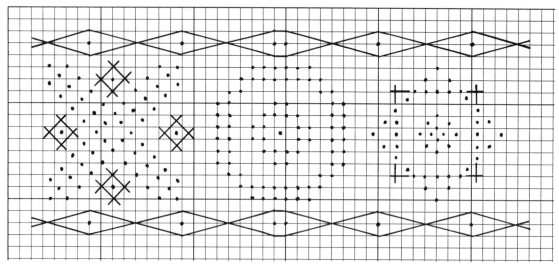

5-20.

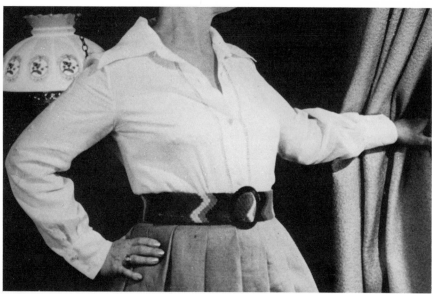

5-21.

Figure 5-20 shows the design that was used to make the candlewick border. Use all three motifs, just one, or make your own design, using the candlewick counterpane shown in figure 3-3 as an inspiration.

Transfer the design by one of the methods suggested in Chapter 1 or try the colonial method described in Chapter 3. Since each diamond on the border is eight inches long, adjust the length at the center or sides of the skirt if necessary.

Complement your beautiful skirt with a white handkerchief-linen blouse. The blouse shown in detail in figure 5-21 exhibits a variety of open-work stitches—ladder hemstitching, buttonhole flower stitch and a blanket-stitch scroll design for the eyelets, and satin-block cutwork—all of which are explained in Chapter 2.

5-22. Eighteenth-century linen petticoat from Vermont, with a crewel-embroidered border. *Courtesy of the Museum of Fine Arts, Boston. Gift of Mrs. Samuel Cabot.*

Skirt With Needlecraft Band

Quilting, patchwork, appliqué, or any other type of embroidery will make a striking band for a skirt—and there's less fabric to handle and decorate. The crewel-embroidered skirt shown in figure 5-22 is a beautiful example of a seventeenth-century petticoat with a band.

Design

The band can be as narrow as six inches or as wide as eighteen inches. Be sure to allow for embroidery "shrinkage" when you cut out the band— two to four inches will be needed, plus three and five-eighths inches for the hem and seam allowance. The strip should be wide enough to be worked on a hoop or frame, so extra fabric will be needed in any case. The appliquéd valance shown in figure 5-31 lost an inch, and an allover quilted band could lose a great deal more.

Center your pattern over the strip, locating the hem edge, and transfer. Stitch the ends of the band in a seam. Complete the needlework, press, and trim the band even if necessary.

Assembly

Follow the basic skirt directions above to estimate yardage, allowing for the band shrinkage and adding the band measurements. If the band becomes narrower than the skirt width, make deeper seam allowances when stitching the skirt seams. Make the hem as directed for the basic skirt, or line the band to the edge with self- or lightweight fabric, before joining it to the skirt. Pin the lining and the band right sides together (figure 5-23). Stitch in a five-eighths-inch seam along the lower (hem) edge (1). Trim the seam, turn the band and the lining right side out, press the hem edge, and baste the upper edges together. Pin the band to the skirt, right sides together, and stitch in a five-eighths-inch seam (2). Press the band down and the seam allowances up and complete the skirt with placket and waistband as for the basic skirt.

5-23.

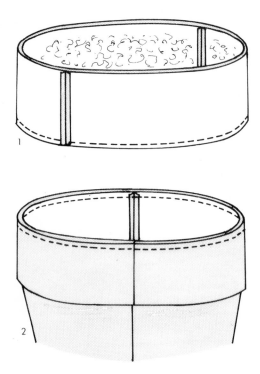

Quilted Skirt

Why not make a quilted skirt or a skirt with a quilted band? The intricately quilted petticoat shown in figure 5-24 was done either on a hoop or in the lap, as the seams were stitched before it was quilted. Today we would call this petticoat a skirt, although here it is an elaborate companion to a wedding dress made of Spitalfields brocade. A farthingale (a series of wire hoops held together with cloth strips and anchored at the waist) was worn under the petticoat to make it stand out.

To make a quilted skirt, follow the basic skirt instructions, adding the batting and a "tube" of lightweight muslin or another fabric for backing. Remember to allow four to six inches for "shrinkage." Finish the hem edge of the skirt with binding (figure 3-20) or a hem.

The homey patchwork "pocket" shown in figure 5-25 was made in the late eighteenth or early nineteenth century from recycled fabric. Why not make one of these as a companion to your skirt? It will hold all your needlework supplies and make you feel at home in a colonial setting.

5-24. Wedding dress of Mary Beck, 1742, brocade with quilted petticoat. *Courtesy of the Museum of Fine Arts, Boston. Photo: Creative Photographers.*

5-25. Patchwork pocket. *Courtesy of the Smithsonian Institution.*

Insertionwork Garments

The beautiful blue satin dress shown in figure 5-26 is just one example of what can be done with insertionwork—you can also try a pair of pants for a change of pace.

Materials

You will need graph paper with one-eighth- to one-quarter-inch grids, a pattern with gores or detailed seams, fabric (the same yardage and notions as specified in the pattern), matching or contrasting embroidery yarn or thread (match the weight of the fabric), and sharp-pointed needles.

Assembly

Predetermine the skirt or pants length, allowing three-quarters inch extra for the hem. Make a graph-paper gauge as explained in Chapter 2 and cut out the garment pieces according to the pattern layout. Matching points cannot be used for insertionwork, so mark each garment piece in the waist seam allowance or on a piece of paper pinned to each section (center front, right front, left front, etc.). Seams to be joined with insertion stitches use the regulation five-eighths-inch seam allowance. When they are turned back three-quarters inch, an opening one-quarter inch wide will be created when the two sections are embroidered together. Hem edges are finished the same way. (Instructions are given in Chapter 2 for a narrow hem held in place by the stitches, which eliminates the handsewn step.)

To make the skirt, put a narrow hem around the side and hem edges of each panel. Work insertion stitches along one seam at a time, reinforcing the bottom edges with French tacks. Use faggoting bundles for the center front and back seams; knotted Cretan insertion, for side front and back seams; and knotted buttonhole stitch, for the side seams, so the stitch can be continued along the side edges of the zipper. Join all the front panels, then all the back panels, with your favorite stitch.

Insert the zipper on the left side *by hand*—zipper teeth are not covered. Place the hemmed side edges of the skirt over the zipper tape, leaving a one-quarter-inch space between the folded edges, and baste. Slip-stitch (figure 3-18) the folded edge to the zipper tape, pulling back the tape ends at the lower end so they won't show. Join both side seams with insertion stitches, basting the graph-paper diagram below the zipper. Attach the waistband as instructed in your pattern. Complete the skirt with knotted blanket stitch (figure 2-56) all around the hem to secure it in place.

Armhole facings were eliminated in the blouse. After stitching the side seams, turn in the armhole edges along the seamline and make a narrow hem. Make openings in the blouse front as instructed in Chapter 2. Faggoting bundles were used down the center front, with knotted buttonhole insertions on each side.

Cut out two complete neck bands and join them at one shoulder seam. Stitch one band along the neck edge, and again one-half inch below the first stitching, leaving an opening for turning. Stitch the other band along the lower edge, leaving openings to insert the neck edges of the blouse, and again one-half inch above the first stitching. Trim and clip the seams, and turn the narrow bands right side out and press. Slip-stitch the opening in the upper band together. Stitch the lower band section to the neck edges and slip-stitch in place on the inside. Trace the neck-band pattern pieces without the seamlines. Baste the two fabric strips to the tracing and use knotted insertion stitch to join the two band sections.

5-26.

Crewelwork Robe

You can capture the elegance of the bed rug shown in figure 3-1 in an off-white wool robe (page 86). The predominant stitch was the graceful chain stitch, using three-ply baby yarn. It was elongated to give the scallops a most unusual effect. The outer edge was worked with two rows of indigo blue and one row of baby blue. The grape outlines were worked first and then filled in. Every motif and branch was outlined with chain stitch. Select your favorite leaf and flower designs, using the bed rug as a guide.

To work out the design for your project, exert a little ingenuity. Work out the pattern (figure 5-27) on tracing paper. The scallops on the robe were traced with a meat platter; a thimble, salt shaker, and bottle caps were used to make the flower and grapes; and the extra curlicues were drawn in. Adapt a design for the corner—this robe has a slanted-front opening edge, so the pattern here is slightly different than on the bed rug.

If you want to use this crewel embroidery on a garment, purchase a roll of tracing paper from an artist-supply store. Trace the pattern pieces and mark the seamlines, symbols, and darts so you know where to end the lines.

Enlarge the design as instructed in Chapter 1. Follow the sequences for the bed rug in Chapter 3, tracing the outline to each pattern piece and adjusting the scallop length if necessary for a continuous outline on your garment. When you transfer your outline to the fabric, be sure to trace along the outer edge of each pattern piece. This will make it easier to cut out the garment and match the embroidered design. Every pattern piece was transferred to the robe fabric and embroidered before the sections were cut out. These preliminary steps will shorten your cutting and sewing time considerably.

5-27.

Rocking-Chair Pads

The sugar-loaf design used for the rocking-chair pads shown in figure 5-28 (and in color on page 85) and for the quilt shown on page 83 is a twelve-inch-square block. For the rocking chair only the patchwork triangle was used from the original quilt block. For the back pad three-and-one-eighth-inch-wide strips were mitered at each edge to fit between the triangles; two-and-one-half-inch mitered strips were used for the seat pad.

Materials

You will need polyester batting; one-quarter yard fabric apiece for patches 1, 2, and 3; three-quarters yard fabric for patch 4; bias binding and tie strings; one-half yard fabric each for patches 5 and 6; and one and one-half yards fabric for the mitered strips and back.

5-28.

128

Pattern

The diamond pattern shown in figure 5-29 is used for patches 1, 2, 3, 4, and 5. It has broken lines in both directions. The shorter line forms patch 6, and the longer line divides the diamond for patches 1, 3, and 5 when they are used to make blocks at each end of the rectangles. Be sure to allow a quarter-inch seam allowance on all edges.

Pattern-layout graphs are shown in figure 5-30. Make a pattern for the back (1) and for the seat (2), adjusting the strip widths to your needs. The chair shown in figure 5-28 required a rectangle nineteen inches by thirty inches for the back and an eighteen-inch square, shaped at the back, for the seat.

5-29.

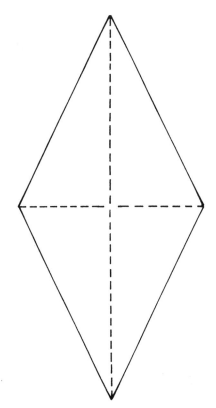

5-30.

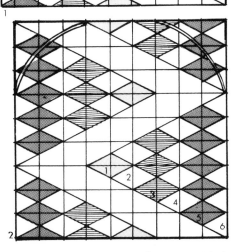

each square = 1 inch

Assembly

Make the patchwork top and assemble the units for quilting. Quilt by hand or by machine, as desired. Cut the bias strips and bind the edges as shown in figure 3-20. Cut four strips, one inch wide and fourteen inches long, for the back (if the top must be tied around a wide strip of wood, adjust the length accordingly), and four strips the same size for the seat. Fold the strips in half lengthwise and stitch in a quarter-inch seam. Turn the strips right side out by attaching a darning needle with heavy thread to the seam allowance at one end. Insert the needle eye first into the tube and work through to the other end, pulling the fabric over the thread as it turns right side out. Sew the strips securely at each corner of the back pad and at the required places for the seat pad (each chair is different).

Muslin Curtains With Appliqué Valance

The lovely window treatment shown in figure 5-31 and in color on page 85 was adapted from the quilt design shown in figure 3-11.

Materials

You will need two and one-half yards medium-weight muslin for the valance and the tie-backs; ten yards gauze muslin for the curtains; one yard green polka-dot fabric for the scroll and the crab-apple leaves; one-half yard red polished cotton for the crab apples; one-half yard solid green cotton for the cherry, strawberry, and grape leaves and stems and the strawberry tops; one-quarter yard dull red cotton for the cherries, strawberries, and pincushion; one-quarter yard solid blue fabric for the grapes; one-half yard calico print for the basket and binding; blue and green cotton embroidery floss for the basket and stems; and double curtain rods.

5-31.

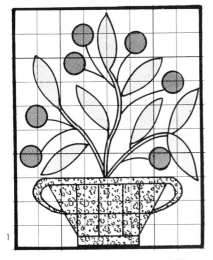

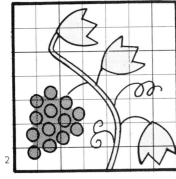

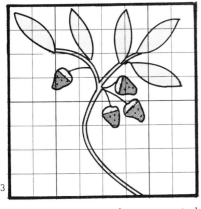

each square = 1 inch

Pattern

The valance pattern was worked out on tracing paper (figure 5-32). The window was seventy-two inches wide, so the design was made twelve inches wide and sixty-four inches long. Only half of the design was drawn. A ten-inch plate was used for the scroll and the end circle, then one-quarter inch was added to each side of the line so the scroll would measure one-half inch wide. Enlarge the basket of cherries (1), the grapes (2), and the strawberries (3) as directed in Chapter 1—the stems on these three patches are one-quarter inch wide. All crab-apple, cherry, and strawberry leaves are the same size on the valance. To enlarge the patterns, make a one-inch circle for the crab apples, a three-quarter-inch circle for the cherries, and a one-and-three-quarter-inch circle for the pincushions at each end. Cut about ten leaves (using the pattern shown in figure 5-33) and ten crab apples from paper and place them around the scroll after the three fruit motifs are drawn in. With this method you can make the design as long and as wide as you wish. You may draw any of the other fruit baskets or designs from the quilt instead of using the three given here.

The valance foundation strip was made fifteen inches wide and ninety inches long for this window. Center the pattern on the fabric strip and transfer the design.

The fruit and pincushion appliqués were stuffed with cotton to create a third dimension. Cut two-and-one-half-inch circles (a demitasse cup was used) for the crab apples; two-inch circles, for the cherries (a salt shaker was this size); and two-and-one-half-inch circles for the pincushion. The strawberry top is green, and the bottom is red. Any of these measurements can be made larger or smaller to suit your design. Cut and press one-inch-wide bias strips for the scroll, and one-half-inch-wide bias strips for the stems, as shown in figure 3-17. Cut as many patches of each as needed for your design, including the basket and the two bunches of grapes and leaves. Transfer each grape outline to the right side of the fabric.

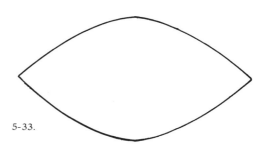

5-33.

Assembly

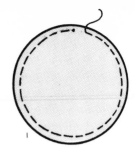

Since the valance was so long, the scroll was slip-stitched (figure 3-18) in place first. Then all the fruit stems were embroidered with chain stitch (figure 2-18), and the leaves were added, again with slip-stitch.

To make the circular patches (figure 5-34), sew a small, evenly spaced running stitch one-eighth inch from the raw edge (1). Pull up the thread to form a pocket and stuff with cotton. The crab apples needed three small cosmetic cotton balls for stuffing, the cherries two, the pincushions six, and the strawberries one. Pull the thread gently until the cut edges meet at the center and fasten securely (2). Slip-stitch the stuffed circles to the foundation. Each grape was stuffed with part of a cotton ball as it was sewn in place. Each grape must be sewn around its outline to separate the bunch (3); it is not necessary to make individual circle patches for each grape. The pincushion was formed by marking off eight sections with green thread. Bring the thread out through the center of the stuffed appliqué, insert it at the edge of the patch on the wrong side, and bring it out through the center, pulling it taut. Space seven more threads equally around the patch, bringing all threads out through the same spot on top. Decorate the center with a one-inch circle of chain stitches (4). The fruit basket was embroidered with blue thread. Chain-stitch all lines and around all edges.

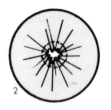

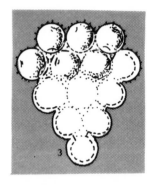

Valance

When the entire design was completed, both the length and the width of the valance foundation shrunk one inch. To make the valance, cut another section fifteen inches by ninety inches for the back. The remaining six-inch strip was used for the tie-backs. Pin the front and back sections right sides together on a flat surface, with the appliquéd section on top. Trim both layers so the edges are straight (figure 5-35). Stitch the end in a half-inch seam, ending two inches from the top edge (1). Press the seam open, continuing across the free edges. Turn in the raw opening edges one-quarter inch, forming narrow hems, and stitch the hems in place (2). Turn the right sides out and press the ends. Baste the raw edges together at top and bottom. Form a casing for the curtain rod by stitching across the valance two inches from the top edge. Encase the raw edges with half-inch-wide bias binding cut from the basket fabric. Cut two-inch-wide strips and bind as shown in figure 3-20.

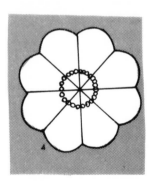

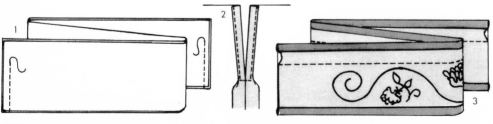

5-35.

Curtains

Cut four equal lengths of gauze muslin. Sew two sections together in a quarter-inch seam along the selvages and press the seams open for each curtain panel. To hem, turn in the sides and the lower two inches and pin. Turn in the selvages and the raw edges one-half inch, forming a one-and-one-half-inch-wide hem, folding in the corners to miter (figure 5-36). Stitch the hems and corners in place (1). To form a casing for the curtain rod, turn the top edge down two and one-half inches. Turn in the raw edge one-half inch, forming a two-inch-wide casing. Stitch the casing edge in place (2).

To make the tie-backs, cut the six-inch strip of fabric in half (forty-five inches each). Fold the tie-backs right sides together and stitch the ends and the long edge in a quarter-inch seam, leaving an opening for turning (3). Turn the right sides out through the opening and press. Slip-stitch the opening shut (4).

5-36.

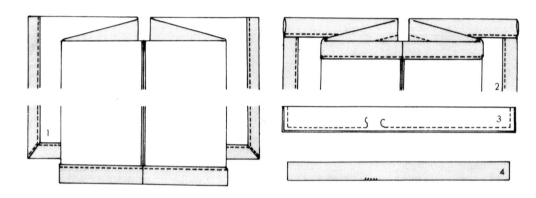

Index